grade **1**

sing a song
of # poetry

A Teaching Resource for Phonemic Awareness, Phonics, and Fluency

1. Make one copy of the poem as a master.

2. Fold the Suggestions up out of sight before making copies for your children.

3. Make copies for children to use in class or share with their families.

This reproducible, one-per-page format enables you to share (when appropriate) printed copies of the poems with your children after you've worked with and enjoyed the poems together in class.

FirstHand
An imprint of Heinemann
A division of Reed Elsevier Inc.
361 Hanover Street
Portsmouth, NH 03801–3912
www.firsthand.heinemann.com

Offices and agents throughout the world

Library of Congress Cataloging-in-Publication Data

CIP data is on file with the Library of Congress.

ISBN 0-325-00656-3

Printed in the United States of America on acid-free paper

07   06   ML   4   5   6

Sing a Song of Poetry

A Teaching Resource for Phonemic Awareness, Phonics, and Fluency

Introduction

Sing a Song of Poetry rolls off the tongue and moves the heart and spirit, if not the feet and hands. Rhythmical language of any sort delights young children as it surrounds them with the magical sounds of dancing words. But poetry, verse, and song provide the magic of teaching as well; indeed, oral language is the doorway to the world of written language and the foundation for literacy. As first graders respond to the sound patterns, intriguing words, and inspiring ideas they find in poems, songs, and rhymes, they are learning invaluable lessons about the ways in which our language works – knowledge that will serve them well as they become readers and writers.

The poems, songs, and rhymes in this volume are a rich source of language, ideas, and imagery that will help first graders use and enjoy oral and written language. This volume is a companion to the lessons described in *Phonics Lessons, Grade 1: Letters, Words, and How They Work* (Pinnell and Fountas 2003, Heinemann). It can also be used as a stand-alone resource for language and literacy opportunities in any primary classroom.

Experiences with poetry help children become aware of the phonological system of language and provide a foundation for matching sounds with letters, letter clusters, and word parts. You can use poems, chants, and songs to help children:

► Listen for and identify rhyming words.

► Identify words with the same beginning, ending, or medial sound.

► Combine sounds to form words and check with the letters.

► Match sounds to letters in words.

► Divide words into separate sounds and match to letters.

Children love poetry with rhythm and rhyme; the language of poetry sings inside their heads. As they grow in experience, they also learn to appreciate poetry that does not rhyme and the sensory images and unique perspectives it evokes. Poetry is related to the many cultures from which children come; by sharing cultures, they construct the common experiences of childhood.

In addition, poetry provides resources for the heart and spirit. Immersing children in simple poetry at an early age helps to instill a lifelong habit of enjoying language and seeking out poetry in order to expand one's vision. Poetry joins us to the past and to our fellow human beings in the present.

VALUES AND GOALS OF POETRY IN THE FIRST GRADE CLASSROOM

Poetry expands children's oral language abilities as it:

- Builds a repertoire of the unique patterns and forms of language.
- Helps children become sensitive to the sounds of language—rhymes, alliteration, assonance, onomatopoeia (*buzz, whiz, woof*).
- Supports articulation and elocution.
- Extends listening and speaking vocabularies.
- Expands knowledge of the complex syntax of language.
- Encourages children to manipulate and play with language.
- Develops phonological awareness (rhyme, syllables, onsets and rimes).
- Develops phonemic awareness (ability to manipulate individual sounds).
- Makes it easy for children to isolate and identify sounds, take words apart, and change sounds in words to make new words.
- Provides rich examples of comparisons such as similes and metaphors.

Poetry expands children's written language abilities as it:

- Provides a setting in which children can develop the concept of a word and notice how spaces are used to define words in written language.
- Gives them access to memorable language that they can then match up with print.
- Provides the opportunity to share in the reading of familiar materials, behaving as readers by following print from left to right and matching word by word.
- Provides a highly supported situation within which they can learn to read and write high frequency words.
- Provides opportunities to connect words by how they sound and look.
- Helps them notice the letters and letter patterns associated with sounds.
- Helps them notice letters that are embedded in words and that words that are embedded in extended text.
- Provides examples of different kinds of words—compound words, base words, contractions, plurals, words with inflectional endings (like *ing, ed*), homophones, homographs, synonyms, and antonyms.
- Provides the opportunities to participate in fluent, phrased reading.

Poetry expands children's content knowledge as it:

- Provides new perceptions and ideas for them to think about.
- Encourages them to develop a sense of humor.
- Sensitizes them to the forms and style of poetry.

Poetry contributes to children's social knowledge and skills as it:

- Provides artistic and aesthetic experiences.
- Creates a sense of community through enjoying rhymes and songs as a group.
- Gives them access to English-speaking culture.
- Provides a common language for a group of children to share.
- Creates memories of shared enjoyable times.

The Elements of Poetry

The following unique elements provide the essence of poetry's appeal. In the poems appropriate for young children, language patterns, rhyme, rhythm, and humor dominate, but all the elements are present.

RHYME

While not all poems rhyme, many of the simple poems children enjoy include words that have alliterative beginning parts (*onsets*) and/or assonant ending parts (*rimes*). The onset of a syllable is the consonant or consonant cluster that starts the word. The rime is the vowel and everything after the first part. So the onset of *duck* is *d* and the onset of *stuck* is *st.* The rime of *duck* is *uck,* and *uck* is also the rime of *stuck.* Words that have the same rime also rhyme. Rhyme is appealing and memorable; rhyme always refers to the sound of the ending part of the word, not necessarily the spelling. Many of us can recall simple rhymes that we learned as children. Notice the rhyme in "Coffee and Tea," even though the words *tea* and *agree* are not spelled the same:

> My sister, Molly, and I fell out,
>
> And what do you think it was about?
>
> She loved coffee and I loved tea.
>
> And that was the reason we couldn't agree.

RHYTHM

Poetry involves both simple and complex rhythms. There is often a "beat" to the language, which, again, makes it memorable and enjoyable, especially when chanted in unison. Take "I Had a Little Brother," for example:

> I had a little brother
>
> No bigger than my thumb;
>
> I put him in the coffee pot
>
> Where he rattled like a drum.

FIGURATIVE LANGUAGE

Poetry often evokes sensory images by making comparisons (similes and metaphors), as in "Snowman":

There is a snowman as round as a ball.

He has two large eyes, but he's not very tall.

If the sun shines down on him tóday,

My jolly snowman will melt away.

Often rhymes, chants, and songs contain onomatopoetic language (words like *whoosh* that sound like the phenomenon they represent). Take this example from "Slip On Your Raincoat":

Slip on your raincoat.

Pull on your galoshes.

Wading in puddles

Making splishes and sploshes.

LANGUAGE PATTERNS

Rhymes and poems are most enjoyable because of the language patterns that are included. *Alliteration*, the repetition of consonant sounds, is evident in "The Big Black Bug":

The big black bug

Bit the big black bear

But the big black bear

Bit the big black bug back!

Children love these tongue twisters, and they are an excellent way to help them internalize initial sounds. Here is another good example:

Fresh fried fish,

Fresh fish fried,

Fried fresh fish,

Fish fried fresh.

Assonance, the repetition of vowel sounds, is evident in the traditional "Moon, Moon":

Moon, moon,

Silvery spoon,

Floating still,

On a night in June.

Moon, moon,

Back too soon,

White and pale

In the afternoon.

REPETITION

Many poems, particularly songs, have repeating stanzas or phrases, such as "Mary Wore a Red Dress." Another example is "The More We Get Together":

Oh, the more we get together,

Together, together,

Oh, the more we get together,

The happier we'll be.

Rhythmic repetition like this helps children learn these rhymes easily; many have been set to music and can be sung, such as "Did You Ever See a Lassie?":

SENSORY IMAGES

Poetry can induce laughter or tears with just a few words because this condensed form of language plays on the senses. Poets evoke memories, form visual images, point up absurdities, and help us enter unique worlds. Christina Rosetti's "Who Has Seen the Wind?" gives us a visual image of the wind:

Who has seen the wind?

Neither you nor I.

But when the trees bow down their heads

The wind is passing by.

Selecting Poetry for Young Children

When using poetry with young children it is helpful to think in terms of the complexity of language and concepts. Also, will the children experience the poems orally or do you expect them to process the print? Children can listen to and recite more complex poems than they can read. Carefully consider the characteristics of the texts you use for shared reading to be sure they are within the range of children's independent reading after many opportunities for shared reading. The first poems children encounter should be very simple in terms of:

▶ Length and number of words.

▶ Decodability.

▶ Ratio of easy to harder high frequency words.

▶ Sentence or phrase structure.

▶ Vocabulary (although children may enjoy many rhymes without knowing the precise meaning of some archaic words, such as "pease porridge").

▶ Ideas; for example, visual imagery and metaphor require more of the child than simple rhymes and songs.

The poems in this book represent a gradient of difficulty. At the beginning of the year, select very simple poems, gradually increasing the level of challenge. The poems in the chart below illustrate a continuum of difficulty.

① SIMPLEST	② MORE DIFFICULT	③ MOST DIFFICULT
Mouse in a Hole	**Six Little Ducks**	**Little Nancy Etticoat**
A mouse lived in a little hole,	Six little ducks that I once knew,	Little Nancy Etticoat
Lived quietly in a little hole.	Fat ones, skinny ones, fair ones too,	With a white petticoat,
When all was quiet, as quiet as can be . . .	But the one little duck	And a red nose;
OUT POPPED HE!	With a feather on his back,	She has no feet or hands,
	He led the others with his	The longer she stands,
	Quack, quack, quack.	The shorter she grows.

Verse 1 is both simple and short. The theme is easy; words are simple with few syllables; there is repetition. Children can say it over and over, substituting other animals. Verse 2 tells a story. The lines are longer and more complex, but the imagery is easy to grasp and the rhythm helps children learn it. Verse 3, "Little Nancy Etticoat," is no longer than "Six Little Ducks," but the theme is more complex and the words more difficult to decode. While the poem has rhythm, it is less pronounced. More thinking is demanded of the reader. Of the three selections, only number three has poetic quality.

As you select poems to share, consider your children's previous experience, skill with language, and vocabulary. If you begin with easy poems and they learn them very quickly (for example, they join in during shared reading and remember them), you can provide slightly more complex examples.

Planning for Teaching Opportunities When Revisiting a Text

As short texts, poems provide a multitude of opportunities for learning about language. After enjoying a poem several times, you may want to revisit the text with children to help them notice letter patterns or make connections between words. The following grid helps you think about the varied opportunities in particular texts. In each box we list possible elements to show, reinforce, or help children notice within a poem. You can try planning some poems out for yourself in advance (see the blank form following the filled-in chart) or use the blank grid to keep a record of your teaching points within each poem as you make them.

WORD ANALYSIS TEACHING OPPORTUNITIES WHEN REVISITING POETRY

Title	Type of Text (e.g., limerick, tongue twister; couplet, free verse)	Phonogram Patterns (e.g., -at, -ig, -oan, -ait, -ate)	Letter-Sound (beginning or ending consonants and clusters)	High Frequency Words	Other (e.g., syllables, contractions, suffixes/inflectional endings, compound words, plurals, ending consonants/clusters/ digraphs, concept words like colors and numbers, names)
The Little Plant	3-verse poem lines 1, 2 and 4 of each verse rhyme	-eed, -eep, -ant, -ine, -ight	h, s, b, l, p, w, v, r, m, f, pl, cr, dr, pl, wh	a, in, the, of, said, and, to, it, see, what	double *t* double *e* compound words
Betty Botter	tongue twister rhythmic, alliterative poem	-utter, -itter, -atter, -ought, -ake, -an, -it, -ill	b, s, m, w, p, th, sh	some, she, but, said, will, and, than, if, of, make, her, bought, this, put	two syllable words, -er ending, assonance (repetition of vowel sounds, double consonants, "twas" meaning "it was"
Apples, Peaches	4-line poem with alternate line rhymes	-ell, -en, -um, -ear, -each	p, t, m, c, y, b	me, when, your, come	concept of fruit compound word (*birthday*) plurals with *s, es*
Are You Sleeping?	song with repetition	-ing, -ong	y, j, m, b, r, d, sl, br	are, you	*ing* ending
Banbury Cross	nursery rhyme with rhyming pairs of lines rhythmic	-an, -ell, -ide, -ing, -ock	b, r, s, f, l, h, t, m, g, cr, sh, wh	to, see, on, her, she, shall, have	double *s*
Bat, Bat	5-line verse with 2 rhyming pairs of lines	-at, -and, -ice, -en, -ake	b, c, m, h, g, y, b, g, n, wh	come, my, and, you, when, if, an, not	contraction (*I'll*) multisyllable words (*bacon, mistaken*)

WORD ANALYSIS TEACHING OPPORTUNITIES WHEN REVISITING POETRY

Title	Type of Text (e.g., limerick, tongue twister, couplet, free verse)	Phonogram Patterns (e.g., -at, -ig, -oan, -ait, -ate)	Letter-Sound (beginning or ending consonants and clusters)	High Frequency Words	Other (e.g., syllables, contractions, suffixes/inflectional endings, compound words, plurals, ending consonants/clusters/digraphs, concept words like colors and numbers, names)

Tools for Using Poetry

The tools for working with poetry are simple. You will want to have them well organized and readily available for quick lessons. We suggest the following:

▶ **EASEL**

a vertical surface for displaying chart paper or the pocket chart that is large enough for all children to see and sturdy enough to avoid tipping.

▶ **POCKET CHART**

a stiff piece of cardboard or plastic that has lines with grooves into which cards can be inserted so that children can work with lines of poems and/or individual words.

▶ **MASKS**

cutout cardboard shapes designed to outline words on charts for children to use in locating words or parts of words (see templates in "Materials and Routines," *Phonics Lessons 1, Teaching Resources*).

▶ **HIGHLIGHTER TAPE**

transparent stick-on tape that can be used to emphasize words, letters, or word parts.

▶ **STICK-ON NOTES**

small pieces of paper that have a sticky backing and can temporarily be used to conceal words or parts of words so that children can attend to them.

▶ **FLAGS**

a handle with a flat piece of wood or cardboard on the end that can be placed under a word on a chart as a way to locate or emphasize it (see templates in "Materials and Routines," *Phonics Lessons, 1, Teaching Resources*).

▶ **TAGS**

signs with concise directions so that children can remember an independent work activity; for example: *Read, Mix, Fix, Read* (*Read* the poem, *Mix* up the sentence strips of a poem, *Fix* the poem back together, and *Read* it again to check it).

▶ **ART MATERIALS**

media such as paint, glue, colored paper, tissue paper.

Instructional Contexts for Poetry

There are several instructional contexts within which you can use rhymes and poems effectively. For more information on instructional practices see Fountas and Pinnell (1996) *Guided Reading: Good First Teaching for All Children* and Pinnell and Fountas (1998) *Word Matters: Teaching Phonics and Spelling in the Reading/Writing Classroom.*

INTERACTIVE READ-ALOUD

Children enjoy hearing poetry read aloud. In addition, reading aloud provides a model of fluent, phrased reading. There are many wonderful picture books that present rhyming verse to children in a very engaging way. *The Itsy Bitsy Spider* (Trapani 1993) is an illustrated variation of the familiar verse. *Pignic* (Miranda 1996) is a wonderful rhyming (and repetitive consonant sounds) alphabet book in which a family of twenty-six pigs have a picnic with all kinds of food. *Chicka Chicka Boom Boom* (Martin and Archambault 1985) is another rhyming alphabet book with wonderful rhythm and a focus on uppercase and lowercase letters. You can also read individual poems from volumes such as *Tomie dePaola's Mother Goose Favorites* (1985).

We recommend repeated readings of favorite poems or rhyming books; it takes many repetitions for children to be able to join in. Ask them to listen the first two or three times you read a verse, but encourage them to join in after they have grasped enough to say it with you, especially on a refrain. In this way, children will begin to internalize much of the language and enjoy it more and will also get the feeling of participating in fluent, phrased reading.

SHARED READING

Shared reading involves children's both hearing the verse and seeing the print. You use an enlarged text—a chart that you have prepared or purchased or a big book. Using this shared approach allows you to demonstrate pointing while reading. After one or two repetitions, encourage children to read with you in an interactive read-aloud. Be sure that all children can see the visual display of print. You'll want to sit or stand to the side and use a thin pointer (pointers that have objects like "hands" on the end usually block children's view of the very word you are pointing out). The idea is to maximize children's attention to the print. Shared reading helps them learn how the eyes work in reading. They'll also learn more about rhyme and rhythm.

CHORAL READING AND PERFORMANCE

Choral reading is a more sophisticated version of shared reading. Participants may read from an enlarged text, but often they have their own individual copies. They may have a leader, but it is not always necessary for the leader to point to the words. Participants can practice reading together several times and then perform the piece. There can be assigned "solo" lines, boys' and girls' lines, question and response lines, or the whole group can read all the lines. Emphasize varying the voice to suit the meaning of the poem. You can add sound effects (wooden sticks, bells, or other simple tools) or simply have children clap or snap their fingers to accentuate words or phrases.

RECITATION

It is very useful for children to commit some poems to memory. Chances are, these poems will stay with them in some form throughout their lives. Choosing a favorite poem and saying it enough times to remember it helps children learn to sustain attention and, again, to internalize rich language. Often, poems expand vocabulary. When poems are memorized, they can be recited for the class or others. This activity shouldn't cause anxiety; you can incorporate it into the classroom matter-of-factly. Let the student choose: this ensures the appropriate level of difficulty, and the task will be more enjoyable.

INDEPENDENT READING

Children love reading poetry, searching for favorite poems, and illustrating poems. A personal poetry book or anthology becomes a treasure. After poems have been read in shared reading, you can reproduce them on smaller pieces of paper. Children glue the poems in a composition book or spiral notebook and illustrate them. Be sure that you are using poems that they are familiar with and can read. Reading their personal poetry books is a good independent reading activity. You can increase the complexity of poems for first graders.

WRITING POETRY

Children can begin to get a feel for writing verse through interactive writing. In interactive writing, you and the children compose a message together. You act as a scribe, using the easel, but occasionally children come up and write in a word or letter when you want to draw attention to it. (See *Interactive Writing: How Language and Literacy Come Together, K–2,* McCarrier, Pinnell, and Fountas 2000)

You can substitute their names in a verse or create a variation of one of their favorites (for example, for "Brown Bear, Brown Bear, What do you see?" substitute "Black Cat, Black Cat, What do you see?"). This activity gives them power over language, and they may want to experiment on their own.

You can also help children see how to create a poem and to realize that a poem does not have to rhyme. In writer's workshop, children may describe an event or scene that lends itself to poetry. You can help them reshape the written piece by taking out unnecessary words and laying it out as a poem. As children hear many examples of poems, they will want to write their own.

Maintaining individual poetry anthologies often prompts children to try writing their own poems on themes and in forms similar to their choices. Encouraging this experimentation helps them use language in new ways.

Types of Poetry

Poetry can be categorized in many different ways—by pattern, structure, or topic, for example. This book includes rhymes and poems under the headings discussed below, which are related to both forms and themes. Many of the poems could be placed in more than one category.

NURSERY RHYMES

Traditional rhymes by anonymous poets have been passed down over generations. There are often many different versions. Originally serving as political satire for adults, they have been loved by children for generations. They usually rhyme in couplets or alternating lines and are highly rhythmic. Young children enjoy these simple verses, and they help to build a foundation that will later lead them to a more sophisticated appreciation of poetry. The "Mother Goose" rhymes, which were published in the eighteenth century, are the best known, but equivalents exist around the world. An example children love is "Hey, Diddle, Diddle,"

Hey, diddle, diddle,

The cat and the fiddle,

The cow jumped over the moon.

The little dog laughed

To see such sport,

And the dish ran away with the spoon.

RHYMED VERSE

Many poems for young children have lines that end with words that rhyme. These may be rhyming couplets (each pair of lines rhyme), as in "What Do You See?"

What do you see?

A pig in a tree.

Where's your cat?

Under my hat.

How do you know?

He licked my toe.

Or, every other line may rhyme, as in "One for the Money":

> One for the money,
>
> Two for the show,
>
> Three to get ready,
>
> And four to go.

There are a variety of other rhyming patterns. You may even see verses where every line rhymes, as in "I Scream":

> I scream.
>
> You scream.
>
> We all scream.
>
> For ice cream!

FREE VERSE (UNRHYMED)

Many poems evoke sensory images and sometimes have rhythm, but do not rhyme. Haiku poems, for example, have a defined number of syllables; these "spare" poems evoke visual images. An example is "Snow" by Issa.

> I could eat it!
>
> This snow that falls
>
> So softly, so softly.

Here's an example of an intriguing verse that has rhythm but does not rhyme—"Ladies and Gentlemen":

> Ladies and gentlemen,
>
> Come to supper—
>
> Hot boiled beans
>
> And very good butter.

WORD PLAY

Some poems play with words by juxtaposing interesting word patterns in a humorous and playful way, like "What's Your Name?"

What's your name?

Puddin' Tame.

Ask me again

And I'll tell you the same.

Where do you live?

In a sieve.

What's your number?

Cucumber!

In word play we also include tongue twisters (poems that play with words in a way that makes them very difficult to recite without stumbling because the words are difficult to pronounce one after another). A well-known example is "Betty Botter":

Betty Botter bought some butter,

"But," she said, "this butter's bitter.

If I put it in my batter,

It will make my batter bitter.

But a bit of better butter

Will make my batter better."

So she bought a bit of butter

Better than her bitter butter,

And she put it in her batter.

So 'twas better Betty Botter

Bought a bit of better butter.

HUMOROUS VERSE

Humorous verse draws children's attention to absurdities as well as to the sounds and rhythms of language. Sometimes these humorous verses tell stories—for example, "There Was an Old Man of Peru":

There was an old man of Peru

Who dreamed he was eating his shoe.

He woke in the night

In a terrible fright,

And found it was perfectly true.

The above verse is a limerick, a highly structured form in which the first two lines rhyme, the second two lines rhyme, and the fifth line rhymes with the first two.

SONGS

Songs are musical texts originally intended to be sung. An example is "I Love the Mountains":

I love the mountains.

I love the rolling hills.

I love the flowers.

I love the daffodils.

I love the fireside

When all the lights are low.

Boom-de-otta, boom-de-otta,

Boom-de-otta, boom-de-otta.

You may know the traditional tunes to the songs we have included in this volume, but if you don't, you can compose your own tune or simply have children chant them, enjoying the rhythm and rhyme.

ACTION SONGS AND POEMS

Action poems involve action along with rhythm and rhyme. An example is "I'm a Little Teapot":

I'm a little teapot,

Short and stout.

Here is my handle. [*One hand on hip*]

Here is my spout. [*Other hand pointed outward*]

When I get all steamed up,

I just shout,

"Tip me over, [*Lean over sideways as if to pour tea*]

And pour me out."

This category also includes jump-rope songs, traditional rhymes that children originally chanted while they jumped rope. An example is "Ball-bouncing Rhymes":

Number one, touch your tongue.

Number two, touch your shoe.

Number three, touch your knee.

Number four, touch the floor.

Number five, dance and jive.

Children can chant and act out jump-rope songs.

There are also chants that accompany games or are simply enjoyable to say together. Chants are like songs in that they have rhythm and rhyme, but they are meant to be spoken in chorus rather than set to music. "Counting Polar Bears," for example, is a fast-moving question and answer chant.

"Hello, hello, hello, sir.

Meet me at the grocer."

"No, sir."

"Why, sir?"

"Because I have a cold, sir."

"Where did you get your cold, sir?"

"At the North Pole, sir."

"What were you doing there, sir?"

"Counting polar bears, sir."

"How many did you count, sir?"

"One, sir; two, sir; three, sir; four, sir;

Five, sir; six, sir; seven, sir; eight, sir;

Nine, sir; ten, sir."

"Good-bye, good-bye, good-bye, sir!

See you next July, sir."

CONCEPT POEMS

Poems in this category focus on concepts such as numbers, days of the week, colors, ordinal words, seasons, and any other category of information. An example is "Traffic Safety":

Red light says stop.

Green light says go.

Yellow says be careful.

You'd better go slow.

When I reach a crossing place,

To left and right I turn my face,

And then I walk, not run, across the street,

And use my head to guide my feet.

These verses are not only engaging but also easy to learn. As children learn them, they will be repeating the vocabulary that surrounds important concepts.

In the category of concept poems, we also include name poems, which really transcend categories. Many verses present a wonderful opportunity to substitute children's names for names or words already there. An example is "Papa's Glasses":

These are Papa's glasses.

This is Papa's hat.

This is how he folds his hands

And puts them in his lap.

Many of the verses in other sections of the book also offer opportunities for similar innovations, so look for opportunities. Children will love substituting their own words and phrases. They will develop ownership for the writing and become more sensitive to rhymes, syllables, and word patterns in the process.

Fifty Ways to Use Poems—Plus!

Below we suggest fifty specific ways to use the poems in this volume. Plus, you will notice that each poem includes an instructional suggestion— an easy way to refine and extend the learning and enjoyment potential of each poem. You will find many more ways to engage your children in joyful play with oral and written language. The rich collection of poems in this volume can be reproduced, analyzed, or simply read aloud. Enjoy!

1. POEMS ON TAPE	Record specific poems on a tape so that children can listen independently at a listening center. Include card stock copies of the poems, and show children how to follow along with the recording.
2. CLASS READINGS OF POEMS ON TAPE	Make a recording of the children saying the poems and have them join in when the tape plays.
3. POEM PICTURES	After reading a poem aloud at different times of the day, have children make pictures to go with it and display them with the poem. Duplicate individual copies of a simple poem and ask each child to illustrate it.
4. WORD ENDINGS	Write the poem in large print on a chart or on strips for a pocket chart. After many readings of a poem on a large chart, help children notice words that rhyme and specific vocabulary. They can use a masking card or highlighter tape to mark these words.
5. POEM INNOVATIONS	Engage children in noticing and using the language syntax in the poem to create their own similar versions. For example, insert different names in "Mary Wore Her Red Dress" or different foods in "Mary Ann, Mary Ann."
6. PERSONAL POETRY BOOKS	Have children make their own personal poetry books by gluing the poems they have experienced in shared reading into spiral notebooks and then illustrating them. Over time they will have a large personal collection of poems to take home.
7. LITTLE POEM BOOKS	Make individual poem books, with one line of a poem on each page (for example, "I Have Two Eyes"); children can illustrate each page, read the book, and take it home.
8. POEM PERFORMANCES	Children can perform the poems after they learn them, sometimes adding sound effects with rhythm instruments such as sticks and drums or by clapping and snapping their fingers.

9. POEM RECITATIONS	Have children learn some favorite poems by heart so that they can recite them independently.
10. POETRY PLAY	Lead children in saying their favorite poems while they line up, as they walk through an area in which their talking will not disturb other classes, or any time they have a moment or two of "wait time."
11. LINE-UP POEMS	When passing out of the room for recess or lunch, play games in which children say or finish a line of a poem in order to take their place in line.
12. POEM CHOIRS	Have children perform as a "voice choir" in which they say parts of poems with expression and/or at various volumes. You can assign "solos," have girls and boys read alternative lines, or introduce other variations.
13. RHYMING CLOZE	Read poems, asking children to join in only on the rhyming words. Put highlighter tape on the rhyming words.
14. FINGER POEMS AND ACTION POEMS	Make finger plays from poems. Do poems with motions involving the entire body. We have included finger-play and action directions for many poems, but you can make up many more.
15. POEM POSTERS	Use art materials (colored and/or textured paper, pens, crayons, paints) to illustrate poems on charts for the whole group to enjoy, or individually in personal poetry books.
16. POEM DISPLAYS	Display a poem in several places in the room; children find the poem and use chopstick pointers to read it in small and large versions in different places.
17. POETRY BOX	Make a poetry box that contains slightly enlarged and illustrated versions of familiar poems; children can take them out and read them to a buddy.
18. POETRY BOARD	Make a theme poetry board using poems that explore a concept (for example, animals or vegetables).
19. TONGUE TWISTERS	Make up tongue twisters using the names of children in the class and have them illustrate the verses; for example *Carol carries cookies, carrots, candy, and cucumbers in a cart.*

20. POCKET CHART	Place poems on sentence strips in a pocket chart for a variety of activities: • Substituting words to innovate on the text; • Highlighting words, letters, or parts of words with colored transparent plastic or highlighter tape; • Putting sentence strips in order and reading; • Masking words; • Placing cards over words to predict and then check predictions with the print.
21. POEM PUZZLES	Have the children cut a poem into strips, mix them up, order them, and glue them on paper in the correct order. Then have them use art materials to illustrate the text. You can create a simple strip template to photocopy for many different poems.
22. PERSONALIZED POETRY	Give children copies of previously shared poems on chart paper. Select poems that have potential for innovation. Leave blanks for children to write in words—their own names or names of friends, favorite colors, numbers, foods, etc. Let them choose words for the blanks and then illustrate the poems.
23. WALL POEMS	Place one or two lines of a poem on separate posters and have children illustrate them. Then mount the posters on the wall. Children can read across the posters, pointing as they go.
24. CONCEPT POEMS	Place poems on particular topics at appropriate places in the classroom. For example, place a poem about windows on the window, one about trees on a window that looks out at a tree, or one about flowers next to a vase of flowers.
25. SEQUENCING POEMS	Give children a poem whose lines have been written on separate pages. Ask them to put the pages in order, staple them together as a book, illustrate the pages, and then read the book to others.
26. MORE SONGS AND POEMS	Be on the alert for popular songs that children like or street rhymes that they know. Take appropriate verses from these songs and add them to the poetry collection.
27. FAVORITE PHRASES/ WORDS IN POEMS	Put a large-print copy of a poem on the wall. Have children choose words or phrases that they love and mark them with highlighter tape. Make a "quotes" poster with several lines all the children know and like to repeat or include in their writing.
28. POEM CARDS	Create a "poem card" on which children keep a list of poems, rhymes, or songs they have learned "by heart." They can set a goal of five to ten poems for the card.

29. POEM PLAYS	Create a "play" from the poem. Read the poem (children may join in) while several children act it out.
30. POETRY DRESS-UP	Collect some simple "dress up" items related to the rhymes and poems in your collection. Invite the children to dress up for the poem reading.
31. POETRY PARTY	Have a party to which everyone comes dressed as a character from a poem. (Props may be made of paper.) The group has to guess which poem is represented and then read the poem to the child representing that character.
32. CHARACTER BULLETIN BOARD	Each child draws a favorite character from a poem and then cuts the figure out. Use interactive writing to create labels for each character on the board.
33. POETRY CIRCLE	Have children sit in a circle so that everyone can see everyone else. Ask each child to read or say a poem of her or his choice.
34. POET OF THE DAY	Each day assign a "poetry leader" who reads or says a poem and/or chooses a poem for the class to read.
35. SING A SONG OF POET-TREE	Have a large tree in the room (real or cardboard). Let every child hang a favorite poem on the tree. Change the poems periodically.
36. PUPPET SHOW	Have the children make and use finger, stick, or hand puppets to say the poem.
37. POETRY AND PROSE	Take a poem and create a "prose" version of it. Place the two versions of the story beside each other so that children can see and talk about differences in language, form, punctuation, mood, etc.
38. POETRY BREAKFAST OR POETRY NIGHT	Schedule a parent-meeting "poetry show." Children can perform poetry in groups or as individuals. Parents can look at their individual poetry anthologies.
39. BORROW FROM A POEM	Invite children to "borrow" a phrase or line from a poem they know and use it as part of their own poem.
40. POETRY PAINTINGS	Have children do a painting to match a poem. Type the poem and place it under each painting. These poetry paintings make a beautiful display for the corridor.

41. POETRY GREETING CARDS	Have children choose a favorite poem, glue it in a folded card, and then illustrate it.
42. TABLEAU	Have groups of children depict a poem as a "frozen" three-dimensional "painting." Let the other children guess the poem represented.
43. POETRY MIME	Have children, without using words, act out a poem individually or as partners. The rest of the class has to guess the name of the poem.
44. POETRY PICNIC	Many poems have something to do with food. For example, "curds and whey" is cottage cheese. After children have learned a lot of verses, make a list of foods. Children can bring some of them or you can bring them. Then, they say the poem and eat the food.
45. POETRY PAIRS	Children find two poems that go together in some way. They bring the two poems to sharing time and tell how they are alike. You can make a class book of poem pairs with (illustrated) connected poems on opposite pages.
46. POETRY LANDSCAPE MURAL	Children paint a background on which they can glue different poetry characters. This mural requires some planning. For example, you would want a field of corn for "Little Boy Blue" or a mountain for the bear to go over.
47. POETRY SORT	Have a box of poems on cards that children know very well and can read. They can read the poems and sort them in any way they want to—theme (happy, silly, sad), topic (mice, girls, boys, bears), the way they rhyme (two lines, every other line, no rhyme).
48. POEMS IN SHAPES	Have children read a poem and then glue the poem on a shape (give them a template) that represents it. For example, "I'm a Little Teapot" could be on a teapot.
49. POETRY NEWSLETTER	Send home a monthly newsletter that tells parents the poems children have learned and provides some poems they can sing or say at home.
50. CLASS POETRY BOOK	Collect favorite poems into a class book that is small enough to be portable. Children take turns taking the book home. They can read the poems to stuffed animal or family members.

Poetry Links to Phonics Lessons

In *Phonics Lessons: Letters, Words, and How They Work, Grade 1,* you will find under LINK, Shared Reading recommendations that enable you to connect learning across the Language and Literacy Framework. Often, the shared reading recommendations suggest you turn to *Sing A Song of Poetry* for instructional follow-up using particular poems, songs, and verse. This list links many phonics lessons to a specific poem that extends and refines the instructional aim of the lesson; however, you will notice that not all lessons are linked to a poem and, sometimes, a lesson is linked to two or more poems. What does this mean? The links are completely flexible! Feel free to find and make your own links, and do not feel compelled to use every poem we recommend.

The primary goal of this collection is, quite literally, to "sing a song of poetry"! Invite your children to chant, recite, echo, and play with the poems. Above all, *Sing A Song of Poetry* is meant to inspire a love of language.

Early Literacy Concepts

ELC 1	Five Little Speckled Frogs; Good Morning, Mrs. Hen	**ELC 3**	The Boy in the Barn; Little Robin Redbreast
ELC 2	A Birthday Song; Going to the Fair	**ELC 4**	I Know a Little Puppy; This Little Hand

Phonological Awareness

PA 1	Ball-bouncing Rhymes; The Clever Hen; Jack-in-the-box	**PA 7**	Five Little Leaves; Handy Pandy
PA 2	Willy Boy, Willy Boy; Wise Old Owl	**PA 8**	I Don't Suppose; I Have Two Eyes
PA 3	Two Little Dogs, Way Down South	**PA 9**	I Never Had a Dog That Could Talk (*pig/jig; tune/moon; had/that*); I Went Downstairs (*flour/flower; sharp/harp*)
PA 4	Little Sally Waters; My Apple		
PA 5	Dingle Dangle Scarecrow; Five Fat Peas	**PA 10**	I Know Something; I Went Downtown
PA 6	"Fire! Fire!" Cried Mrs. McGuire; Fishy-fishy	**PA 11**	Sing, Sing; A Snail

Letter Knowledge

LK 1	Jack Be Nimble; Little Peter Rabbit; Mary Wore Her Red Dress	**LK 8**	I've Got a Dog as Thin as a Rail; Merrily We Roll Along
LK 2	Slip on Your Raincoat; Three Elephants	**LK 9**	Five Little Sparrows; I Don't Suppose
LK 3	Mary Wore Her Red Dress; Polly Put the Kettle On	**LK 10**	1, 2, 3; Aunt Maria
LK 4	Little White Rabbit; Moon, Moon	**LK 11**	Nut Tree; Three Jolly Gentlemen
LK 5	What Do You See?; Where, Oh, Where Has My Little Dog Gone?	**LK 12**	Mouse in a Hole; My Bike
		LK 13	Monday Morning; Out
LK 6	A Snail; The Vowel Song	**LK 14**	
LK 7	The Moon Shines Bright; Slowly, Slowly	**LK 15**	Old Dan Tucker; Tommy Snooks

Letter/Sound Relationships

LS 1	Bat, Bat; Bears Eat Honey	**LS 11**	The Squirrel; Three Elephants
LS 2		**LS 12**	Away Down East, Away Down West; Bat, Bat
LS 3	Betty Botter; The Big Black Bug; Swim, Swan, Swim	**LS 13**	Five Little Sparrows; Mary's Canary
LS 4	Jack Sprat; Johnny Appleseed	**LS 14**	Roosters Crow; There Was an Old Man of Peru
LS 5	The Boy in the Barn; The Elephant Who Jumped a Fence	**LS 15**	Alice, Where Are You Going?; There's Music in a Hammer
LS 6	Listen to the Tree Bear; Six Little Ducks	**LS 16**	
LS 7	Auntie, Will Your Dog Bite?; Choo-choo Train	**LS 17**	Can You Wash Your Father's Shirt?; Slip on Your Raincoat
LS 8	The Old Woman; Soda Bread	**LS 18**	The Clever Hen; Dingle Dangle Scarecrow
LS 9	Six Little Snowmen; A Snail; The Itsy, Bitsy Spider	**LS 19**	I Know Something; One, Two, Three, Four, Five
LS 10	A Cloud; A Horse and a Flea and Three Blind Mice; Slowly, Slowly	**LS 20**	Old Mother Hubbard; The Queen of Hearts
		LS 21	Alice, Where Are You Going?; One, Two, How Do You Do?

Spelling Patterns

SP 1	Fishy-fishy; Mary Ann, Mary Ann; Thank You
SP 2	I Know Something; Little Sally Waters; My Favorite Toys
SP 3	I Had a Little Rooster; Sam, Sam, the Butcher Man
SP 4	Hickory, Dickory, Dean; I've Got a Dog as Thin as a Rail
SP 5	Apples and Bananas; My Bike
SP 6	Fishy-fishy; Mary Ann, Mary Ann

SP 7	A Horse and a Flea and Three Blind Mice; The Old Man and the Cow
SP 8	Aunt Maria; Chitterabob
SP 9	I Know Something; I Went Downtown
SP 10	The Lady and the Crocodile; Mary Had a Little Lamb

High Frequency Words

HF 1	All By Myself; Colors; Lavender's Blue
HF 2	I Have Two Eyes; My Aunt Jane
HF 3	My Big Ballon; My Bike
HF 4	My Favorite Toys; The Old Gray Cat
HF 5	Papa's Glasses; Saturday Night

HF 6	Polly Put the Kettle On; Pumpkin Orange
HF 7	Coffee and Tea; Roosters Crow
HF 8	Say and Touch; Sing a Song of Sixpence

Word Meaning

WM 1	Monday Morning; There Are Seven Days
WM 2	My Big Balloon; A Tiny Seed

WM 3	Apples, Peaches; Cap, Mittens, Shoes, and Socks

Word Structure

WS 1	My Favorite Toys; The Smile Song
WS 2	Six Little Ducks; Three Elephants
WS 3	Apples, Peaches, Five Little Sparrows; Papa's Glasses
WS 4	Baby Bumblebee; Willy Boy, Willy Boy
WS 5	Choo-choo Train; Five Enormous Dinosaurs; Five Little Leaves; She'll be Coming 'Round the Mountain
WS 6	The Elephant Who Jumped a Fence; On Top of Spaghetti

WS 7	Pumpkin Orange; What's Your Name?
WS 8	Baby Rhinoceros; The Grand Old Duke of York; I Would If I Could
WS 9	"Fire! Fire!" Cried Mrs. McGuire; If You're Happy and You Know It; It's Raining, It's Pouring; The Pussycat and the Queen; Shoo Fly
WS 10	Snowman; Two Cats of Kilkenny

Word Solving Actions

WSA 1	A Cloud; Six Little Snowmen
WSA 2	Five Little Mice; Four Seasons
WSA 3	Esau; How Much Dew?; Jack Sprat
WSA 4	The Elephant Who Jumped a Fence; I Had a Loose Tooth
WSA 5	Little Bird; The Little Plant
WSA 6	I'm a Little Teapot; Johnny Appleseed
WSA 7	My Hat, It Has Three Corners; The Old Gray Cat
WSA 8	The Old Man and the Cow; The Old Woman
WSA 9	The Donkey; Six Little Snowmen

WSA 10	Hey Diddle Diddle Dout; A Snail
WSA 11	A Tiny Seed; What Do You See?
WSA 12	Baby Rhinoceros; The Gingerbread Man
WSA 13	Going to the Fair; I Had a Little Rooster
WSA 14	Hanky Panky; Here We Go
WSA 15	Hickory, Dickory, Dare; I Don't Suppose
WSA 16	I Have a Little Cough; I Went Downtown
WSA 17	Little Bo-Peep; The Lion and the Unicorn
WSA 18	The More We Get Together; My Love for You

1, 2, 3

1, 2, 3

Father caught a flea.

Put him in a teapot,

To drink a cup of tea.

1, 2, 3

SUGGESTION: This nonsense rhyme presents a funny situation. Have children read the rhyme at a fast pace and then talk about how a flea could possibly drink a cup of tea. After children know the poem, you can revisit it to look at words with *ea*.

A-hunting We Will Go

Oh, a-hunting we will go,

A-hunting we will go,

We'll catch a little fox,

And put him in a box,

And then we'll let him go.

SUGGESTION: After the children learn this song, ask them to come up with other animal names and objects that rhyme, such as: *cat–hat; fish–dish; bear–chair; whale–pail; skunk–trunk; snail–jail.*

Alice the Camel

Alice the camel has five humps.

Alice the camel has five humps.

Alice the camel has five humps.

So ride, Alice, ride.

Boom, boom, boom, boom!

SUGGESTION: Children love to perform this countdown song as a group. In the second verse, Alice has four humps and then three humps, and so forth. Everyone gathers in a circle with their arms around the shoulders of the children next to them. As they sing/say the three lines per verse about how many humps the camel has, they bend down at the knees and bounce. As they sing/say the *Boom, boom…* lines, they bump hips with the children next to them (carefully). When "no humps" is reached, change the last line to: *'Cause Alice is a horse, of course*.

Alice, Where Are You Going?

Alice, where are you going?

Up the stairs to take a bath.

Alice with legs like toothpicks

And a neck like a giraffe.

Alice stepped in the bathtub.

Alice pulled out the plug.

Oh my goodness!

No control!

There goes Alice down that hole.

Alice?

Alice?

Gurgle, gurgle, glug.

SUGGESTION: Have the children read the last line slowly and say each word a little softer.

All by Myself

Hat on head, just like this,
Pull it down, you see.
I can put my hat on
All by myself, just me.

One arm in, two arms in,
Buttons, one, two, three.
I can put my coat on
All by myself, just me.

Toes in first, heels down next,
Pull and pull, then see,
I can put my boots on
All by myself, just me.

Fingers here, thumbs right here,
Hands warm as can be.
I can put my mittens on
All by myself, just me.

SUGGESTION: Perform this poem as a play, a different child acting out each verse using actual clothing (or just pantomiming putting on the garments). Make a shared-writing list of all the things children can do by themselves, and invite them to illustrate it.

The Alphabet Song

A – B – C – D – E – F – G,

H – I – J – K – L – M – N – O – P,

Q – R – S,

T – U – V,

W – X,

Y and Z.

Now I've said my ABCs.

Tell me what you think of me.

I think you're wonderful!

SUGGESTION: Say the last line loudly. You can also change the song to sing the alphabet backward.

The Ants Go Marching

The ants go marching one by one,
Hurrah, hurrah.
The ants go marching one by one,
Hurrah, hurrah.
The ants go marching one by one,
The little one stops to have some fun.
And they all go marching down,
To the ground,
To get out,
Of the rain.
BOOM! BOOM! BOOM! BOOM!

ADDITIONAL VERSES:
two by two . . . tie his shoe
three by three . . . climb a tree
four by four . . . shut the door
five by five . . . take a dive
six by six . . . pick up sticks
seven by seven . . . yell out seven
eight by eight . . . shut the gate
nine by nine . . . check the time
ten by ten . . . say "The End!"

SUGGESTION: You can sing this song to the tune of "When Johnny Comes Marching Home." Emphasize the word *down* and then use a mechanical repetitive tone (like a drum) for lines ending with *down*, *ground*, and *rain*. Say the last line loudly.

Apples and Bananas

I like to eat eat eat apples and bananas.
I like to eat eat eat apples and bananas.

I like to ate ate ate ay-ples and bay-nay-nays.
I like to ate ate ate ay-ples and bay-nay-nays.

I like to eat eat eat ee-ples and bee-nee-nees.
I like to eat eat eat ee-ples and bee-nee-nees.

I like to ite, ite, ite, i-ples and bi-ni-nis.
I like to ite, ite, ite, i-ples and bi-ni-nis.

I like to ote ote ote o-ples and bo-no-nos.
I like to ote ote ote o-ples and bo-no-nos.

I like to ute ute ute u-ples and bu-nu-nus.
I like to ute ute ute u-ples and bu-nu-nus.

Now we're through, through, through, through,
Now we're through with the apples and bananas,
Now we're through, through, through, through,
With a, e, i, o, and u.

SUGGESTION: This is a playful song with a catchy chant. The words change to reflect long vowel sounds. Children catch on to this singing game and enjoy making up their own verses featuring other foods.

Apples, Peaches

Apples, peaches,

Pears, plums,

Tell me when your

Birthday comes.

SUGGESTION: Chant this song while going around a circle. Each child takes a turn saying the month or the day and month of his or her birthday.

Are You Sleeping?

Are you sleeping, are you sleeping,

Brother John? Brother John?

Morning bells are ringing,

Morning bells are ringing,

Ding, ding, dong,

Ding, ding, dong.

FRENCH TRANSLATION:
Frère Jacques, Frère Jacques,
Dormez-vous? Dormez-vous?
Sonnez les matines,
Sonnez les matines,
Din, din, don,
Din, din, don.

fold
here

SUGGESTION: This simple song is a good one to help children learn a "round." Have half the class start to sing the song. The rest starts the song when the first group finishes line 2.

40

Aunt Maria

Aunt Maria, she sat on the fire.

The fire was too hot, she sat on the pot.

The pot was too round, she sat on the ground.

The ground was too flat, she sat on the cat.

The cat ran away with Maria on her back.

SUGGESTION: Substitute first and last names of children in the class. Have children highlight simple phonograms such as *-at* and *-ot*.

fold here

41

Auntie, Will Your Dog Bite?

Auntie, will your dog bite?

No, child, no!

Chicken in the bread tray,

Making up dough.

Auntie, will your oven bake?

Yes, just try!

What's that chicken good for?

Pie! Pie! Pie!

Auntie, is your pie good?

Good as you can expect!

Chicken in the bread tray,

Peck! Peck! Peck!

fold
here

SUGGESTION: Assign individual children to read the questions while the rest of the class chants the answers.

42

Away Down East, Away Down West

Away down east, away down west,

Away down Alabama,

The only girl that I like best,

Her name is Susie Anna.

I took her to a ball one night

And sat her down to supper.

The table fell and she fell too

And stuck her nose in the butter.

The butter, the butter,

The yellow margarine.

Two black eyes and a jelly nose

And all the rest turned green.

SUGGESTION: After they are familiar with the poem, divide the children into three groups and have each group read a verse.

Baby Bumblebee

I'm bringing home a baby bumblebee.

Won't my mother be so proud of me?

I'm bringing home a baby bumblebee.

Ouch! He stung me!

ADDITIONAL VERSES:
I'm talking to my baby bumblebee.
Won't my mother be so proud of me?
I'm talking to my baby bumblebee.
"Oh," he said, "I'm sorry."

I'm letting go my baby bumblebee.
Won't my mother be so proud of me?
I'm letting go my baby bumblebee.
Look! He's happy to be free!

SUGGESTION: Children will enjoy pretending to have a trapped bumblebee. You may want to use only the first verse until children know it. They can whisper during the second stanza.

Baby Rhinoceros

We're bringing home a baby rhinoceros.

Won't our mothers be so proud of us?

'Cause we're bringing home a baby rhinoceros.

Oops! He swallowed us!

ACTIONS:

We're bringing home a baby rhinoceros. [*children are in a line with both hands over one shoulder as if dragging something heavy*]

Won't our mothers be so proud of us?

'Cause we're bringing home a baby rhinoceros.

Oops! He swallowed us! [*children fall on the floor*]

SUGGESTION: This adaptation of the "Baby Bumblebee" is good for group enactment as indicated in the actions above. Everyone in the class can participate if there is room. You may want to have children scrunch down into a ball on the floor instead of falling if the room is crowded.

Ball-bouncing Rhymes

Number one, touch your tongue.

Number two, touch your shoe.

Number three, touch your knee.

Number four, touch the floor.

Number five, dance and jive.

Number six, pick up sticks.

Number seven, say eleven.

Number eight, shut the gate.

Number nine, touch your spine.

Number ten, do it all again!

SUGGESTION: Have the class chant these rhymes as different children bounce a ball and perform the actions. Toss the ball to student number one, who bounces it once and performs the indicated action. This child passes or tosses the ball to student number two, who bounces it twice, performs the indicated action, and then passes the ball to student number three, and so on, through student number ten. Repeat until everyone has had a turn.

Banbury Cross

Ride a cockhorse

To Banbury Cross,

To see a fine lady

Upon a white horse.

Rings on her fingers

And bells on her toes,

She shall have music

Wherever she goes.

SUGGESTION: This poem has a very bouncy rhythm. The words mimic the sound of hoofbeats. Children may clap the beat by tapping hands or fingers on their palms. Different groups of children may read each line. Discuss which lines of the poem suggest the clearest mental image: the cockhorse (rocking horse), the fine lady, the white horse, the rings and bells the lady is wearing?

fold here

47

Bat, Bat

Bat, bat, come under my hat,

And I'll give you a slice of bacon.

And when I bake,

I'll give you a cake,

If I am not mistaken.

SUGGESTION: This poem has infectious rhymes and humorous imagery. Invite the children to substitute other *b* words for *bat*, such as *bird* or *butterfly*—or *bumblebee*!

Bears Eat Honey

Bears eat honey.

Cows eat corn.

What do you eat

When you get up in the morn?

Monkeys eat bananas.

Cows eat corn.

What do you eat

When you get up in the morn?

Horses eat oats,

Cows eat corn,

What do you eat

When you get up in the morn?

SUGGESTION: Use interactive writing to create an answer to each verse: cereal, pancakes, oatmeal. Later, use these items to create more verses.

Bees

If bees stay at home,

Rain will soon come.

If they fly away,

Fine will be the day.

SUGGESTION: Discuss the idea that bees might fly to gather pollen when the sun is shining brightly. Children may notice that *home* and *come* look the same at the end but don't rhyme but that *away* and *day* both look the same and rhyme.

Betty Botter

Betty Botter bought some butter,

"But," she said, "this butter's bitter;

If I put it in my batter,

It will make my batter bitter.

But a bit of better butter

Will make my batter better."

So she bought a bit of butter

Better than her bitter butter,

And she put it in her batter.

So 'twas better Betty Botter

Bought a bit of better butter.

SUGGESTION: Have the children read this verse slowly several times, then increase their speed on subsequent readings—without mispronouncing the words! Explain that *'twas* is short for *it was*.

fold
here

51

A Bicycle Built for Two

Daisy, Daisy, give me your answer true.

I'm half crazy all for the love of you.

It won't be a stylish marriage.

I can't afford a carriage.

But you'll look sweet, upon the seat

Of a bicycle built for two.

SUGGESTION: Children are probably not familiar with this song. Teach it to them and sing it together. A bicycle built for two may be a new concept for many children. Before discussing the idea in depth, invite children to draw, dictate, or write about what a bicycle built for two might look like. Share and discuss these ideas; if possible, share a drawing or photograph of the real thing.

The Big Black Bug

The big black bug

Bit the big black bear,

But the big black bear

Bit the big black bug back!

SUGGESTION: Children will enjoy learning and practicing this tongue twister. Have them practice saying the verse slowly at first and increasing their speed on rereadings. You may want to support them by presenting one line at a time and having them repeat it back to you. You can also use this in a pocket chart and substitute words (*brown* for *black*) as the children become faster when reciting it.

A Birthday Song

_____ has a birthday.

We're so glad!

We hope that _____ birthday

Is the best _____ ever had!

SUGGESTION: Make this a traditional birthday ritual for each child in the class. Let children with summer birthdays pick a day in April or May. Make it on chart paper, or in a pocket chart, so it can be revisited often. Be sure to point out that the third line changes (*his, her*) accordingly.

The Boy in the Barn

A little boy went into a barn,

And lay down on some hay.

An owl came out and flew about,

And the little boy ran away.

SUGGESTION: Some children may need some background on what a barn is and why there might be hay and an owl there.
Have children discuss why the boy might have run away.

fold
here

55

Bumblebee

Bumblebee was in the barn,

Carrying dinner under his arm.

Buzzzzzzz-zz-z!

ACTIONS:
Bumblebee was in the barn, [*circle finger in the air*]
Carrying dinner under his arm. [*move finger close to arm*]
Buzzzzzzz-zz-z! [*poke arm*]

SUGGESTION: Children will enjoy this nonsense poem. You may want to call attention to the word *buzz* and discuss the
idea that this word actually sounds like the noise the bee makes.

Bunch of Blue Ribbons

Oh, dear, what can the matter be?

Oh, dear, what can the matter be?

Oh, dear, what can the matter be?

Johnny's so long at the fair.

He promised to buy me a bunch of blue ribbons,

He promised to buy me a bunch of blue ribbons,

He promised to buy me a bunch of blue ribbons,

To tie up my bonny brown hair.

SUGGESTION: Children can substitute different colors for the ribbons. Use this poem in a pocket chart and substitute the color words. You may want to explain that *bonny* is another word for *pretty*.

Can You Can?

Can you

Can a can

As a canner

Can can

A can?

SUGGESTION: Have children highlight or underline the word *can*, including part of the word *canner*. Discuss the two meanings of *can*.

Can You Wash Your Father's Shirt?

Can you wash your father's shirt,

Can you wash it clean?

Can you wash your father's shirt,

And bleach it on the green?

Yes, I can wash my father's shirt,

And I can wash it clean.

I can wash my father's shirt,

And send it to the Queen.

SUGGESTION: Have half the children read the first verse and the other half read the second; invite the children to imagine what the line *bleach it on the green* might mean. Explain that the *green* would be a lawn and that the sunshine will remove color or *bleach* something.

Cap, Mittens, Shoes, and Socks

Cap, mittens, shoes, and socks,

Shoes and socks.

Cap, mittens, shoes, and socks,

Shoes and socks.

And pants and belt, and shirt and tie,

Go together wet or dry,

Wet or dry!

SUGGESTION: Have the children sing the rhyme to the tune of "Head, Shoulders, Knees, and Toes." After they are familiar with the words, you could sing the song by dropping off one word each time you repeat the verse—children either say nothing in place of that word, hum, or clap.

Catalina Magnalina

She has a peculiar name but she wasn't to blame,

She got it from her mother, who's the same, same, same.

Chorus

    Catalina Magnalina, Hootensteiner Bogentwiner

    Hogan Logan Bogan was her name.

She had two peculiar teeth in her mouth,

One pointed north and the other pointed south, south,

    south.

Chorus

She had two peculiar eyes in her head,

One was purple and the other one was red, red, red.

Chorus

SUGGESTION: Sing the song to the tune of "There Was a Crooked Man." You may want to clap the four-syllable words in the chorus. Explain to children what a chorus is (sometimes known as a refrain).

fold
here

61

Chitterabob

There was a man,

And his name was Dob.

And he had a wife,

And her name was Mob.

And he had a dog,

And he called it Cob.

And she had a cat,

Called Chitterabob.

"Cob," says Dob.

"Chitterabob," says Mob.

Cob was Dob's dog,

Chitterabob Mob's cat.

SUGGESTION: Children will love learning and practicing this tongue twister. After they are familiar with the words, try dividing the group in two and ask them to alternate lines as they recite—one group makes a statement and the other responds with the follow-up line, providing more information.

Choo-choo Train

This is a choo-choo train,

Puffing down the track.

Now it's going forward,

Now it's going back.

Now the bell is ringing,

Now the whistle blows.

What a lot of noise it makes

Everywhere it goes.

SUGGESTION: Line up your class and have children hop aboard as the train leaves the station. Recite the poem together while you all move down the track. Add puffing, chugging, and choo-choo sounds, even a bell or train whistle. Pair this verse with Eve Merriam's picture book *Train Leaves the Station*.

fold
here

63

The Clever Hen

I had a little hen,

The prettiest ever seen.

She washed the dishes

And kept the house clean.

She went to the mill

To fetch some flour.

She brought it home

In less than an hour.

She baked some bread,

And took in the mail.

She sat by the fire,

And told many a fine tale.

SUGGESTION: After children are familiar with this verse you may want to introduce the talking mother from "Good Morning Mrs. Hen" (also in this volume). You could also pair this rhyme with the classic folktale *The Little Red Hen*, illustrated by Paul Galdone. (For an updated version try *The Little Red Hen Makes a Pizza*, by Philemon Sturges.)

The Clock

There's a neat little clock,

In the schoolroom it stands,

And it points to the time

With its two little hands.

And may we, like the clock,

Keep a face clean and bright,

With hands ever ready

To do what is right.

SUGGESTION: After children know the poem, you may want to talk about the comparisons in it—a person's face and hands with the clock's face and hands.

fold
here

65

A Cloud

What's fluffy white and floats up high,

Like a pile of cotton in the sky?

And when the wind blows hard and strong,

What very gently floats along?

What brings the rain, what brings the snow,

That showers down on us below?

When you look up in the high blue sky,

What is that thing you see float by?

A cloud!

ACTIONS:
What's fluffy white and floats up high, [*point skyward*]
Like a pile of cotton in the sky?
And when the wind blows hard and strong, [*wiggle fingers moving horizontally*]
What very gently floats along?
What brings the rain, what brings the snow, [*open hands palm up*]
That showers down on us below? [*wiggle fingers moving downward*]
When you look up in the high blue sky, [*look up*]
What is that thing you see float by?
A cloud!

SUGGESTION: You may want to present this poem (without the title and last line) as a riddle, having children predict the answer. They can also think of other things (besides cotton) that clouds remind them of or make a web of words related to clouds (drawing from the poem).

Cock-a-doodle-doo!

Cock-a-doodle-doo!

My dame has lost her shoe.

My master's lost his fiddling stick,

And doesn't know what to do.

Cock-a-doodle-doo!

What is my dame to do?

Till master finds his fiddling stick,

She'll dance without her shoe.

SUGGESTION: Create some rhythmical sound to accompany *Cock-a-doodle-doo* by inviting some of the children to tap sticks, shake a tambourine, or ring bells.

Coffee and Tea

My sister, Molly, and I fell out,

And what do you think it was about?

She loved coffee and I loved tea,

And that was the reason we couldn't agree.

SUGGESTION: Substitue *My friend* _____ on the first line. Discuss "falling out" as "arguing." Have partners substitute other foods for coffee and tea, providing a good chance for children to create contrasts. Don't worry too much about preserving the rhyme on the last two lines; children will enjoy manipulating the language.

Colors

Red and yellow, pink and green,

Orange and purple, and blue,

I can see a rainbow,

See a rainbow,

See a rainbow too.

SUGGESTION: After children are familiar with the rhyme, have them work in groups of seven to perform the verse for the rest of the class. As they recite, those wearing the particular color step forward as it is spoken. They could also find or make something of that color to hold up as they recite. You might also consider presenting this verse in a pocket chart in order to support children as they choose other colors to substitute.

fold
here

69

Counting Polar Bears

"Hello, hello, hello, sir.

Meet me at the grocer."

"No, sir."

"Why, sir?"

"Because I have a cold, sir."

"Where did you get your cold, sir?"

"At the North Pole, sir."

"What were you doing there, sir?"

"Counting polar bears, sir."

"How many did you count, sir?"

"One, sir; two, sir; three, sir; four, sir;

Five, sir; six, sir; seven, sir; eight, sir;

Nine, sir; ten, sir."

"Good-bye, good-bye, good-bye, sir!

See you next July, sir."

SUGGESTION: Children may perform this verse in two groups, or two children may enact the parts of the polar bear and the person (or animal, there are all kinds of possibilities here) with whom it is talking. Let children take the lead and figure it out their way. Say the chant quickly, picking up the pace on the count.

Crocodile

If you should meet a crocodile,

Don't take a stick and poke him.

Ignore the welcome of his smile,

Be careful not to stroke him,

For as he sleeps upon the Nile,

He gets thinner and thinner.

Remember when you meet a crocodile,

He's looking for his dinner.

SUGGESTION: Compare this poem with "The Lady and the Crocodile" (in this volume). You may want to point out that the Nile is a river.

fold
here

71

Did You Feed My Cow?

Did you feed my cow?
Yes, ma'am!
Will you tell me how?
Yes, ma'am!
What did you feed her?
Corn and hay.
What did you feed her?
Corn and hay.

Did you milk her good?
Yes, ma'am!
Did you milk her like you should?
Yes, ma'am!
How did you milk her?
Swish, swish, swish!
How did you milk her?
Swish, swish, swish.

SUGGESTION: After children have heard the poem and are familiar with the question-and-answer format, you may want to ask the questions and have children respond in unison with their lines. Invite some of the children to read the questions; have the rest of the class respond. Discuss when it would be appropriate to change *ma'am* to *sir*. Having the poem in a pocket chart can make the substitution easy.

Dig a Little Hole

added stanzas by Kate Roth

Dig a little hole.
Plant a little seed.
Pour a little water.
Pull a little weed.

Chase a little bug.
Heigh-ho, there he goes!
Give a little sunshine.
See the little rose!

Dig another hole.
Plant another seed.
Pour some more water.
Pull another weed.

Chase another bug.
Heigh-ho, there he goes!
Give some more sunshine.
See another rose!

SUGGESTION: Ask children for their recommendations on adding actions or movements. This poem can also be the basis for a great mural. Put the stanzas on butcher paper and invite the children to make cut- or torn-paper illustrations. Move the pieces around until the group is satisfied with the arrangement before gluing them down. Children can then stand in front of the mural and recite the poem while they perform the appropriate actions.

Dingle Dangle Scarecrow

When all the cows were sleeping
And the sun had gone to bed,
Up jumped the scarecrow
And this is what he said:

Refrain

    "I'm a dingle dangle scarecrow
    With a flippy floppy hat!
    I can shake my arms like this,
    I can shake my legs like that!"

When the cows were in the meadow
And the pigeons in the loft,
Up jumped the scarecrow
And whispered very soft:

Refrain

When all the hens were roosting
And the moon behind a cloud,
Up jumped the scarecrow
And shouted very loud:

Refrain

SUGGESTION: There's a lot going on in this poem about a scarecrow who waits until farm creatures are sleeping and then scares them! Children will need to hear the poem several times to understand all the things that are happening. This story poem is a great one to stage, with parts for cows, pigeons, hens, and one "dingle dangle scarecrow" who comes to life, shakes his arms and legs, and flippy flops his hat. Other animals may be added as well. Remind children that a *refrain* is similar to a *chorus*.

The Donkey

I saw a donkey

One day old,

His head was too big

For his neck to hold;

His legs were shaky

And long and loose,

They rocked and staggered

And weren't much use.

ADDITIONAL VERSE:
He tried to gambol
And frisk a bit,
But he wasn't quite sure
Of the trick of it.
His queer little coat
Was soft and gray,
And curled at his neck
In a lovely way.

SUGGESTION: This poem evokes an image of a newborn animal. Most children will not have seen a newborn animal but can imagine a tiny donkey with curly fur just learning to walk. They can talk about what the donkey might look like. If you present the second verse, point out that *gambol* and *frisk* have similar meanings—to skip around playfully.

Down on the Farm

Refrain

    Oh, we're on our way, we're on our way to the farm,

    We're on our way, we're on our way to the farm,

    farm.

Down on the farm there is a big brown cow.

Down on the farm there is a big brown cow.

The cow, she makes a sound like this: Moo! Moo!

The cow, she makes a sound like this: Moo! Moo!

Refrain

Down on the farm there is a little red hen.

Down on the farm there is a little red hen.

The hen, she makes a sound like this: Cluck, Cluck!

The hen, she makes a sound like this: Cluck, Cluck!

Refrain

SUGGESTION: Substitute a variety of other animals and the sounds they make such as: *big black dog—Bow-wow! big brown horse—Neigh! Neigh!*

The Elephant Who Jumped a Fence

I asked my mother for fifty cents

To see an elephant jump a fence.

He jumped so high, he reached the sky,

And didn't get back till the Fourth of July.

I asked my mother for fifty more

To see the elephant scrub the floor.

He scrubbed so slow he stubbed his toe,

And that was the end of the elephant show.

SUGGESTION: Children may perform the poem using a paper fence and an elephant cutout or puppet. It's fun to imagine an elephant flying, and children enjoy attending to the rhyming words in a variety of ways—clapping, snapping, shouting, tapping. There are two other "elephant" rhymes in this volume. After the class has enjoyed the jumping elephant who scrubs floors, introduce them to other elephants in "Way Down South" and "Three Elephants."

Engine, Engine, Number Nine

Engine, engine, number nine,

Running on Chicago line.

See it sparkle, see it shine.

Engine, engine, number nine.

Toot-toot! Toot-toot!

Engine, engine, number nine,

Running on Chicago line.

If the train should jump the track,

Do you want your money back?

Toot-toot! Toot-toot!

SUGGESTION: Children can substitute any two- or three-syllable city name for *Chicago*. They can clap the names to see if they will fit. Invite children to sit in a line, locomotive style, and rock forward and backward to the rhythm of the train. Add some instruments—bell, train whistle, and so forth—to go along with *Toot-toot*!

Esau

I saw Esau sawing wood,

And Esau saw I saw him.

Though Esau saw I saw him saw,

Still Esau kept on sawing!

SUGGESTION: Have the children think about which syllables or words to stress and which ones to run together to convey the correct meaning as they read the poem. Talk about the two meanings of *saw* in the poem. Discuss why *sawing* would be related to the act of using a saw to cut wood.

"Fire! Fire!" Cried Mrs. McGuire!

"Fire! Fire!"
Cried Mrs. McGuire.
"Where? Where?"
Asked Mrs. Blair.
"All over town!"
Said Mrs. Brown.
"Get some water!"
Cried her daughter.
"We'd better jump!"
Said Mrs. Grump.
"That would be silly,"
Replied Mrs. Minelli.
"What'll we do?"
Asked Mrs. LaRue.
"Turn in the alarm,"
Said Mrs. Parm.
"Save us! Save us!"
Screamed Mrs. Davis.

The fire department
Got the call,
And the firemen saved them,
One and all!

SUGGESTION: Children can take turns reading the dialogue of each character in this story poem. The whole group can read the last triumphant stanza. To scaffold the learning of second-language students, use this poem with the picture book *"Fire! Fire!" Said Mrs. McGuire*, by Bill Martin Jr.

Fishy-fishy

Fishy-fishy in the brook,

Daddy caught him with a hook,

Mama fried him in the pan,

And baby ate him like a man.

SUGGESTION: Tap a rhythm stick to give a steady beat while the children read the verse. This simple poem tells a story and could be reproduced as a four-page book that children can illustrate and read. They can substitute other names for *Daddy*, *Mama*, and *baby*.

fold
here

Five Bananas

Five bananas on a banana tree,

Three for you and two for me.

Five bananas on a banana tree

Oh! I love those bananas!

Four bananas on a banana tree,

Two for you and two for me.

Four bananas on a banana tree

Oh! I love those bananas!

ADDITIONAL VERSES:

Three bananas on a banana tree,
Two for you and one for me.
Three bananas on a banana tree
Oh! I love those bananas!

Two bananas on a banana tree,
One for you and one for me.
Two bananas on a banana tree
Oh! I love those bananas!

One banana on a banana tree,
Half for you and half for me.
One banana on a banana tree
Oh! I love those bananas!

No bananas on the banana tree,
None for you and none for me.
No bananas on the banana tree
Oh! We have no bananas!

SUGGESTION: This is a good poem to use in a pocket chart, substituting the number words in each stanza. Practice addition and subtraction equations using bananas and other fruit; children can write the equations on the board. Invite your class to hold up the right number of fingers as they say each number word. Other visuals may be used, such as a feltboard with cutout bananas or a whiteboard with banana cutouts held on with two-sided tape.

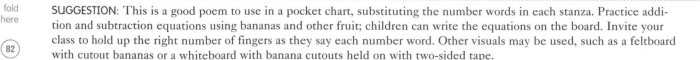

Five Enormous Dinosaurs

Five enormous dinosaurs,
Letting out a roar—
One went away, and
Then there were four.

Four enormous dinosaurs,
Crashing down a tree—
One went away, and
Then there were three.

Three enormous dinosaurs,
Eating tiger stew—
One went away, and
Then there were two.

Two enormous dinosaurs,
Trying hard to run—
One went away, and
Then there was one.

One enormous dinosaur,
Afraid to be a hero—
He went away, and
Then there was zero.

SUGGESTION: Use a magnetic board or feltboard to take away dinosaurs visually.

Five Fat Peas

Five fat peas in a pea pod pressed,

One grew, two grew, and so did the rest.

They grew and grew and did not stop,

Until one day the pod went POP!

SUGGESTION: Children love this infectious counting rhyme and the images of peas growing and the pea pod popping. Invite your class to clap when the pod "POPS"!

Five Little Chickadees

Five little chickadees peeping at the door,

One flew away and then there were four;

Chickadee, chickadee, happy and gay,

Chickadee, chickadee, fly away.

ADDITONAL VERSES:
Four little chickadees sitting on a tree …

Three little chickadees looking at you …

Two little chickadees sitting in the sun …

One little chickadee sitting there as one,
It flew away and then there was none …

SUGGESTION: Invite five children to stand in front of the whole class and "fly away" one by one as the verses are recited.

Five Little Firefighters

Five little firefighters standing in a row;
One, two, three, four, five, they go.
Hop on the engine with a shout,
Quicker than a wink the fire is out!

Four little firefighters standing in a row;
One, two, three, four, whoosh! they go.
Hop on the engine with a shout,
Quicker than a wink the fire is out!

Three little firefighters standing in a row;
One, two, three, whoosh! whoosh! they go.
Hop on the engine with a shout,
Quicker than a wink the fire is out!

ADDITIONAL VERSES:
Two little firefighters standing in a row;
One, two, whoosh! whoosh! whoosh! they go.
Hop on the engine with a shout,
Quicker than a wink the fire is out!

One little firefighter standing in a row;
One, whoosh! whoosh! whoosh! whoosh! she goes.
Hop on the engine with a shout,
Quicker than a wink the fire is out!

No little firefighters standing in a row;
Whoosh! whoosh! whoosh! whoosh! whoosh!

SUGGESTION: Use this verse as a finger play or invite children to act out the poem. They love to be one of the firefighters hopping on board the fire truck and then dropping off one by one as the rest of the class chants the words. You might also consider putting this poem on a chart and with each verse cover an additional number word with *whoosh!* Pair this poem with the picture book *Firefighters A to Z*, by Chris Demarest.

Five Little Froggies

Five little froggies sitting on a well,

One looked up and down she fell.

Froggies jumped high,

Froggies jumped low,

Four little froggies dancing to and fro.

SUGGESTION: After children are familiar with the verse, they can use it as a countdown rhyme. Have five children act out the poem. The rest of the group can recite the poem. You can increase the numbers to include more children in the acting and make the countdown more complex.

fold
here

87

Five Little Leaves

Five little leaves so bright and gay

Were dancing about on a tree one day.

The wind came blowing through the town,

Oooooo . . . oooooo.

One little leaf came tumbling down.

SUGGESTION: Create a very windy classroom by asking the children to make arm motions and "oooo" sounds to represent leaves blowing in the wind. As children become familiar with the words, you can use this verse as a countdown rhyme. Five students may represent leaves, with one "tumbling" off the tree at the end of each stanza as the class recites and makes the appropriate movements and sounds. At the end, the last line changes to: *The last little leaf came tumbling down.* You can also vary the poem's last line to say *The first, The second,* and so forth.

Five Little Mice

Five little mice came out to play,

Gathering crumbs along the way.

Out came pussycat sleek and fat,

Four little mice went scampering back.

ACTIONS:

Five little mice came out to play, [*hands behind back*]

Gathering crumbs along the way. [*one hand comes out with fingers wiggling*]

Out came pussycat sleek and fat, [*other hand comes out cupped like a mouth*]

Four little mice went scampering back. [*both hands behind back—quickly*]

SUGGESTION: You can use this rhyme as a hand play (see Actions above) or choose five mice and one cat to act out the poem as the class recites. One mouse disappears each stanza, until no little mice scamper anywhere.

Five Little Sparrows

Five little sparrows
High in a tree.

The first one says,
"What do I see?"

The second one says,
"I see the street."

The third one says,
"And seeds to eat."

The fourth one says,
"The seeds are wheat."

The fifth one says,
"Tweet, tweet. Tweet, tweet."

SUGGESTION: The whole class can play the role of narrator while five different children read the dialogue. After children know the poem, they can locate words with *ee*.

Five Little Speckled Frogs

Five little speckled frogs

Sitting on a speckled log

Eating some most delicious bugs.

Yum! Yum!

One jumped into the pool

Where it was nice and cool.

Now there are four little speckled frogs.

Burr-ump!

SUGGESTION: Continue this countdown poem with four more verses, beginning with one fewer frog each time. Children will vie to be one of the five speckled frogs who eat delicious bugs and jump in the pool. This is a great game song to sing or recite. In the end there are no more little speckled frogs, and the game can start again.

Four Seasons

Spring is showery, flowery, bowery.

Summer is hoppy, croppy, poppy.

Autumn is wheezy, sneezy, freezy.

Winter is slippy, drippy, nippy.

SUGGESTION: Invite children to talk about how the words describe the seasons and why they might have been chosen. You may need to explain that *bowery* refers to trees. Have the children illustrate the various seasons, relying on the descriptions given in the poem.

Fresh Fried Fish

Fresh fried fish

Fish fresh fried,

Fried fresh fish,

Fish fried fresh.

SUGGESTION: Have children say the tongue twister slowly at first and then faster. After they know the poem and are looking at a written version, have them compare words that start with *f* and *fr*.

fold
here

93

Giddyup, Horsie

Giddyup, horsie, to the fair.

What'll we buy when we get there?

A penny apple and a penny pear

Giddyup, horsie, to the fair.

Up the wooden hill to Blanket Fair,

What shall we have when we get there?

A bucket full of water, a pennyworth of hay,

Giddyup, horsie, all the way.

SUGGESTION: Talk with children about how people used to ride horses to town instead of driving or taking buses. Ask them to guess what *pennyworth* might mean.

The Gingerbread Man

Smiling girls, rosy boys,

Come and buy my little toys;

Monkeys made of gingerbread,

And sugar horses painted red.

SUGGESTION: Have the children clap, snap, or whisper the rhyming words.

fold
here

95

Go 'Round and 'Round the Village

Go 'round and 'round the village,
Go 'round and 'round the village,
Go 'round and 'round the village,
As we have done before.

Go in and out the window,
Go in and out the window,
Go in and out the window,
As we have done before.

Stand and face your partner,
Stand and face your partner,
Stand and face your partner,
As we have done before.

Follow him [her] to London,
Follow him [her] to London,
Follow him [her] to London,
As we have done before.

Now shake his [her] hand and leave him [her],
Now shake his [her] hand and leave him [her],
Now shake his [her] hand and leave him [her],
As we have done before.

SUGGESTION: Have the children stand in a circle. One child is "it" and runs around the circle while the others sing. On the second verse, the children in the circle raise their arms to make windows, and "it" runs in and out between them. On the third verse, "it" chooses a partner and they both bow. On the fourth verse, the partners join hands and skip around the circle. They go back inside the circle on the fifth verse, shake hands, and bow, and the class starts again with a new child chosen to be "it."

Going to the Fair

I know where I'm going.

I'm going to the fair

To see a pretty lady

With flowers in her hair.

So shake it, _____, shake it.

Shake it if you can.

Shake it like a milkshake.

Shake it if you can.

SUGGESTION: Children form a circle and sing the first verse. If you use the second verse, tap one child on the shoulder to stand in the middle and dance, returning to the circle quickly as verse one starts again. You can choose to insert a child's name where the blank line appears or just add an additional *shake it*.

fold here

97

Good Morning, Mrs. Hen

Good morning, Mrs. Hen,

How many chickens have you got?

Madam, I've got ten;

Four of them are yellow,

Four of them are brown,

And two of them are speckled red,

The nicest in the town.

SUGGESTION: Divide the children into two groups to read the parts of Madam and Mrs. Hen. Explain that *Madam* means *Mrs.* or *lady*. You can make this poem interesting by playing with the numbers. Children can work with ten eggs on a felt-board or magnet board, making different combinations that add up to ten. You might want to consider pairing this with "The Clever Hen" (also in this volume).

Good Morning Song

Good morning, good morning, good morning to you,

Good morning, good morning, good morning to you,

Our day is beginning, there's so much to do,

So, good morning, good morning, good morning to you.

SUGGESTION: Use this song as a routine "good morning" song. It will take only a few minutes. After they learn the song, first graders can *read* it in print. You can help them notice the *ing* words.

The Grand Old Duke of York

Oh, the grand old duke of York,

He had ten thousand men.

He marched them up to the top of the hill,

And marched them down again.

Oh, when you're up, you're up,

And when you're down, you're down,

And when you're only halfway up,

You're neither up nor down.

fold
here

SUGGESTION: This is a good marching song. Children can march in place as they recite the first verse. During the second verse, they can match actions to the words line by line: stand up, crouch down, stand halfway up, and then jump up and down.

Handy Pandy

Handy Pandy, Jack-a-dandy,

Loves plum cake and sugar candy.

He bought some at the grocer's shop

And out he came, hop, hop, hop.

VARIATIONS:
Handy Pandy, Jack-a-dandy,
Loves carrot cake and chocolate candy.
He bought some at the grocery store
And he was happy ever more.

Handy Pandy, sugar candy,
French almond rock;
Bread and butter for your supper
That is all your mother's got.

SUGGESTION: There are some great food words in this poem: *plum cake, French almond rock*, and so on. Enjoy saying them together, and illustrate some for a poetry chart. Present the variations and then ask children what they would buy at the grocery store.

Hanky Panky

Down by the banks of the Hanky Panky,

Where the bullfrogs jump from bank to banky

With an Eep! Eep! Ope! Ope!

Knee-flop-i-dilly and kerplop!

SUGGESTION: Children enjoy the nonsense words in this verse. Help them discuss how words can make you think of real noises by suggesting the sounds they represent, such as *purr, buzz, fizz,* and *crackle.*

Hark, Hark!

Hark, hark! The dogs do bark,

Beggars are coming to town;

Some in rags, some in tags,

And some in velvet gowns.

SUGGESTION: Assign four different groups of children one line each. You may want to explain that *beggars* sometimes meant people who dress up and give performances.

Here We Go

Here we go up, up, up,

And here we go down, down, downy

And here we go backwards and forward

And here we go round, round, roundy.

SUGGESTION: Children will enjoy acting out the movements as they recite this simple verse. Starting in a crouching position, they stand up; crouch or sit down; walk backwards and forwards; and then turn around. This can be a quick, yet fun transition verse also. Just announcing "Here we go" when it is time to transition will get their attention and allow them to get ready for a quick chant together. It's also great to revisit when looking at high frequency words or categorizing directional words.

Hey Diddle Diddle

Hey diddle diddle,

The cat and the fiddle,

The cow jumped over the moon;

The little dog laughed

To see such sport,

And the dish ran away with the spoon.

SUGGESTION: This rhyme is an all-time favorite and a great one to act out with stick puppets. Divide the group in half and have each group read three lines. Or have all the children read lines 1 and 2 and assign specific children to read lines 3, 4, 5, and 6. Children will enjoy illustrating the poem as a mural or a four-page book (p. 1—lines 1 and 2; p. 2—line 3; p. 3—lines 4 and 5; p. 4—line 6).

Hey Diddle Dout

Hey diddle dout,

My candle's out,

My little maid's not at home;

Saddle the hog,

And bridle the dog,

And fetch my little maid home.

SUGGESTION: Invite some of the children to beat out the rhythm with a stick or drum while the others say the rhyme.

Hickory, Dickory, Dare

Hickory, dickory, dare,

The pig flew up in the air.

The man in brown

Soon brought him down,

Hickory, dickory, dare.

SUGGESTION: Children will enjoy comparing this poem to "Hickory, Dickory, Dock" and "Hickory, Dickory, Dean"—the events as well as the characters and words.

fold here

107

Hickory, Dickory, Dean

Hickory, dickory, dean,

The dog was very clean.

The cat was fine

To sit and dine,

Hickory, dickory, dean.

SUGGESTION: If you use all three versions ("Hickory, Dickory, Dock;" "Hickory, Dickory, Dean;" and "Hickory, Dickory, Dare"), you can discuss how changing the ending part of a word makes a new word.

Hickory, Dickory, Dock

Hickory, dickory, dock,

The mouse ran up the clock.

The clock struck one

The mouse did run,

Hickory, dickory, dock.

SUGGESTION: This poem lends itself to accompanying actions—the motion of the pendulum (*hickory, dickory, dock*), the mouse running up and down the clock (fingers running up an arm), holding up one finger as the clock strikes one, and then the final back-and-forth pendulum motion. Children can create new verses by changing the time: *The clock struck two. / The cat ran, too.*

Hippity-hop to the Candy Shop

Hippity-hop to the candy shop,

To buy a stick of candy.

One for you, and one for me,

And one for brother Andy.

SUGGESTION: The strong rhythm in this nursery rhyme will make everyone want to go "hippity-hopping." Have children tap rhythm sticks or paper towel rolls to the beat as they sing or chant this verse. Let children think of all the places they could hippity-hop and what they would do when they got there. Substitute the words *my friend* for *brother* and other children's names that end with the long *e* sound. (Or you can change almost any name into a diminutive by adding the long *e* sound.)

A Horse and a Flea and Three Blind Mice

A horse and a flea and three blind mice

Sat on a curbstone eating ice.

The horse he slipped and sat on the flea.

The flea said, "Whoops, there's a horse on me!"

SUGGESTION: Children will enjoy the funny images in the poem. Emphasize expression in saying the last line. You can also point out the quotation marks and exclamation point and discuss what they indicate.

fold
here

111

Horsie, Horsie

Horsie, horsie, don't you stop,

Just let your feet go clippety clop.

Your tail goes swish and the wheels go 'round,

Giddyup, you're homeward bound.

SUGGESTION: Children can come up with the sound effects and motions for this poem: tapping fingernails or clapping for *clippity clop*, moving hands quickly for *swish*, and revolving both hands around each other to show how the *wheels go 'round*. Have children locate words that sound like real noises.

How Much Dew?

How much dew

Does a dewdrop drop

If dewdrops

Do drop dew?

They drop the dew

That they do,

When dewdrops

Do drop dew.

SUGGESTION: Talk about dewdrops and help children notice dew in the morning (a picture would help). Even if they don't fully understand the concept, children can enjoy the nonsense. Compare *do* and *dew*. If children enjoy the tongue twister, introduce them to others in this volume ("I Saw a Saw" and "Peter Piper" are two examples).

fold
here

113

I Don't Suppose

I don't suppose

A lobster knows,

The proper way

To blow his nose.

Or else perhaps,

Beneath the seas,

They have no need,

To sniff and sneeze.

SUGGESTION: It will be interesting to talk about how a lobster could possibly blow his nose. This poem provides a good opportunity to compare homophones (*nose* and *knows*), to notice *ee* and *ea* words, or to locate *sn* clusters.

I Had a Little Brother

I had a little brother

No bigger than my thumb;

I put him in the coffee pot

Where he rattled like a drum.

SUGGESTION: Say the poem with strong rhythm and a fast pace. Children may be interested to notice that *thumb* and *drum* rhyme but that they look different at the end. You can also have them locate double consonants.

fold
here

115

I Had a Little Rooster

I had a little rooster by the barnyard gate,
That little rooster was my playmate.
That little rooster went cock-a-doodle-doo,
Dee-doodle-dee, doodle-dee, doodle-dee-doo.

I had a little cat by the barnyard gate,
That little cat was my playmate.
That little cat went meow, meow, meow,
That little rooster went cock-a-doodle-doo,
Dee-doodle-dee, doodle-dee, doodle-dee-doo.

I had a little dog by the barnyard gate,
That little dog was my playmate.
That little dog went arf, arf, arf,
That little cat went meow, meow, meow,
That little rooster went cock-a-doodle-doo,
Dee-doodle-dee, doodle-dee, doodle-dee-doo.

SUGGESTION: This cumulative story poem could be the basis for a great production number. Individual children are assigned to make the sounds of different animals as the whole group recites or sings the rest of the story. The longer the song, the more it stretches the memory by adding animals.

I Had a Loose Tooth

I had a loose tooth,
A wiggly, jiggly loose tooth.
I had a loose tooth,
A-hanging by a thread.

I pulled my loose tooth,
My wiggly, jiggly loose tooth.
Put it 'neath my pillow,
And then I went to bed.

The fairy took my loose tooth,
My wiggly, jiggly loose tooth.
And now I have a quarter,
And a hole in my head.

ACTIONS:

I had a loose tooth,
A wiggly, jiggly loose tooth. [*pretend to wiggle a tooth as if it were in the mouth*]
I had a loose tooth,
A-hanging by a thread. [*hold hand up as if holding a tooth on a string*]

I pulled my loose tooth, [*pretend to pull tooth*]
My wiggly, jiggly loose tooth. [*pretend to shake tooth in palm of hand*]
Put it 'neath my pillow,
And then I went to bed. [*put two hands together and lean head on them*]

The fairy took my loose tooth, [*pretend to hold up tooth*]
My wiggly, jiggly loose tooth. [*pretend to shake tooth in palm of hand*]
And now I have a quarter, [*hold palm out*]
And a hole in my head. [*point to jaw*]

SUGGESTION: Losing a tooth is a big event in a primary classroom. Children are compelled to talk about the experience, to demonstrate how the tooth finally fell out. Revisit this poem, and the accompanying actions, each time a child loses a tooth. Revisit the poem to notice double consonants and vowels, as well as the *ly* endings.

I Have a Little Cough

I have a little cough, sir,

In my little chest sir,

Every time I cough, sir,

It leaves a little pain, sir,

Cough, cough, cough, cough,

There it is again, sir.

SUGGESTION: Children will have fun acting out the repetitive coughing action in this simple verse. After they are familiar with the words and have had fun with the coughing, it might be a good opportunity to very briefly discuss *sir* and *ma'am*. With the verse on chart paper, or in a pocket chart, you can replace *sir* with *ma'am* and recite the new version together.

I Have Two Eyes

I have two eyes to see with,

I have two feet to run,

I have two hands to wave with,

And nose I have but one.

I have two ears to hear with,

And a tongue to say "Good day."

ACTIONS:
I have two eyes to see with, [*children are sitting; point with both hands to eyes*]
I have two feet to run, [*lift one foot, then the other*]
I have two hands to wave with, [*wave with both hands*]
And nose I have but one. [*point to nose*]
I have two ears to hear with, [*both hands behind ears*]
And a tongue to say "Good day." [*stand up on "Good day"*]

SUGGESTION: Give children reproducible copies of the poem and have them draw a self-portrait to illustrate it. They have to be sure to include everything mentioned in the poem.

I Know a Little Puppy

I know a little puppy; he hasn't any tail.

He isn't very chubby; he's skinny as a rail.

Although he is a puppy, he'll never be a hound.

They sell him at the shop for 30 cents a pound.

Bow-wow, wow-wow, wow-wow, wow.

HOT DOG!

SUGGESTION: This poem is really a riddle. Keep the last two lines covered. After the first four lines, have children guess what kind of "dog" is in the poem, and uncover the last two lines to check predictions. They can talk about the two meanings of "dog."

I Know Something

I know something I won't tell.

Three little monkeys in a peanut shell.

One can read and one can write,

And one can fly a great big kite.

SUGGESTION: Make a triptych by folding a piece of paper into thirds. Children love illustrating one monkey in each space. This poem leaves lots of room for both "monkeyshines" and creative and imaginative thought.

I Love the Mountains

I love the mountains.

I love the rolling hills.

I love the flowers.

I love the daffodils.

I love the fireside

When all the lights are low.

Boom-de-otta, boom-de-otta,

Boom-de-otta, boom-de-otta.

SUGGESTION: This song can be sung as a "round," with one group starting after the other group has sung the first two lines. You can also have two groups sing or say alternate lines, following quickly along. You can have one group say *Boom-de-otta* continually while the others sing the whole song. Pair this verse with the picture book *I Love the Mountains*, by John Archambault.

I Never Had a Dog That Could Talk

I never had a dog that could talk,

Or a cat that could sing a song,

Or a pony that could on two legs walk,

And keep it up all the day long;

Or a pig that could whistle a merry tune,

Or a hen that could dance a jig,

Or a cow that could jump clear over the moon,

Or a musical guinea pig.

SUGGESTION: Invite children to talk about what makes this poem funny. They can substitute names of other animals or their pets or think of other funny characteristics.

I Saw a Saw

I saw a saw in Arkansas,

That would outsaw

Any saw I ever saw,

And if you have a saw

That will outsaw the saw

I saw in Arkansas

Let me see your saw.

SUGGESTION: Invite children to think about the two meanings of the word *saw*. (They may not know the "saw" as a tool.) It will also be interesting to them that *Arkansas* rhymes with *saw* but is spelled differently.

I Saw Three Ships

I saw three ships come sailing by,
Come sailing by, come sailing by;
I saw three ships come sailing by,
On New Year's Day in the morning.

And what do you think was in them then,
Was in them then, was in them then?
And what do you think was in them then,
On New Year's Day in the morning?

Three pretty girls were in them then,
Were in them then, were in them then,
Three pretty girls were in them then,
On New Year's Day in the morning.

And one could whistle and one could sing,
And one could play the violin;
Such joy there was at my wedding,
On New Year's Day in the morning.

SUGGESTION: Substitute current holidays (Valentine's Day, etc.). Children love reciting this poem, as well as illustrating it. They can make a poetry chart for each stanza, adding their own cutout drawings to the printed text. This is a good project for group work.

fold
here

125

I Scream

I scream,

You scream,

We all scream

For ice cream!

SUGGESTION: Compare the words *I scream* and *ice cream*. Have children discuss how thinking about the meaning helps with spelling. Invite children to create, paint, or draw their own incredible ice-cream concoctions.

I Went Downtown

I went downtown
To see Mrs. Brown.

She gave me a nickel
To buy a pickle.

The pickle was sour,
She gave me a flower.

The flower was dead,
She gave me a thread.

The thread was thin,
She gave me a pin.

The pin was sharp,
She gave me a harp.

And the harp began to sing—

Minnie and a minnie
And a ha ha ha!

SUGGESTION: This poem reinforces rhyming words. Children can predict each new item given by Mrs. Brown based on
the word at the end of the preceding line, as well as create their own rhymes. Ask class members to read the first and last
verses together, but divide up the group to read other verses.

I Would If I Could

I would

If I could!

But I can't,

So I won't!

SUGGESTION: This poem doesn't rhyme but depends on rhythm and juxtaposition of words for its appeal. Children will enjoy reciting it emphatically. They can play a game in which one child poses a question (such as *Would you like to eat worms?*) and the rest say the poem as an answer.

If I Had a Donkey

If I had a donkey and he wouldn't go,

Do you think I'd whip him?

Oh, no, no!

I'd put him in the barn,

And give him some corn,

The best little donkey that ever was born.

SUGGESTION: Talk with children about the days when people depended on horses and donkeys to carry them and pull
carts. You could whip your animal or treat it kindly. In this poem, the writer wants to treat the donkey well.

If You're Happy and You Know It

If you're happy and you know it,

Clap your hands.

If you're happy and you know it,

Clap your hands.

If you're happy and you know it,

Then your face will surely show it.

If you're happy and you know it,

Clap your hands.

SUGGESTION: Do the actions while singing or saying the poem. Children enjoy making up new rhymes and motions together, such as *Stomp your feet*, *Stand and cheer*, and *Shout hooray!*

I'm a Little Teapot

I'm a little teapot,

Short and stout,

Here is my handle,

Here is my spout.

When I get all steamed up,

I just shout:

Tip me over

And pour me out!

ACTIONS:
I'm a little teapot,
Short and stout,
Here is my handle, [*one hand on hip*]
Here is my spout. [*other hand pointed outward*]
When I get all steamed up,
I just shout:
Tip me over [*lean sideways to "pour" from spout*]
And pour me out!

SUGGESTION: Many children may already know this old favorite and will enjoy singing it while they act it out. Share a printed version, and have them highlight all the rhyming *-out* words. You can discuss how changing the beginning part of a word makes a new word.

It's Raining

It's raining, it's pouring,

The old man is snoring;

He went to bed and bumped his head

And couldn't get up in the morning.

SUGGESTION: This traditional verse has a somewhat mournful tone, but children enjoy saying or singing it. Revisit the poem on days when the weather matches. You can tag two more lines on the end: *Rain, rain, go away. / Come again some other day.*

The Itsy, Bitsy Spider

The itsy, bitsy spider

Climbed up the waterspout.

Down came the rain

And washed the spider out.

Out came the sun

And dried up all the rain.

And the itsy, bitsy spider

Climbed up the spout again.

ACTIONS:

The itsy, bitsy spider [*touch fignertips of both hands—little fingers to thumbs*]
Climbed up the waterspout. [*walk hands up by changing fingers and thumbs*]
Down came the rain [*make rain motions by fluttering fingers down*]
And washed the spider out.
Out came the sun [*hands above head making a circle*]
And dried up all the rain.
And the itsy, bitsy spider [*repeat spider walking motion*]
Climbed up the spout again.

SUGGESTION: Sing the song with actions. You can have children substitute other words for *itsy, bitsy* that mean *small*, for example: *eensy, weensy; teeny, tiny;* or *wee, little.*

I've Got a Dog as Thin as a Rail

I've got a dog as thin as a rail,

He's got fleas all over his tail;

Every time his tail goes flop,

The fleas on the bottom all hop to the top.

SUGGESTION: This verse has a predictable structure children can use to create other rhymes: *I've got a* _____, *as* _____ *as a* _____. See what your children can come up with, and have them make an illustrated class book to showcase their efforts.

Jack Be Nimble

Jack be nimble,

Jack be quick,

Jack jump over

The candlestick.

Jack be nimble,

Quick as a fox,

Jack jump over

This little box.

ADDITIONAL VERSES
Jack be nimble,
Jack cut a caper,
Jack jump over
This piece of paper.

Jack be nimble,
Jack be fair,
Jack jump over
This little chair.

SUGGESTION: Children enjoy discovering the meaning of the word *nimble*. Class members may take turns jumping over a real or imaginary candlestick. (Candlesticks are easily made from small paper plates, short paper rolls, glue, and paper scraps.) A set of blocks or other obstruction can be jumped instead. Different names could be substituted for *Jack*. Create some new verses in which the second and fourth lines rhyme. Outside, let class members chant the words and jump over a rope held by two children. If everyone makes it over one height, raise the rope.

Jack Sprat

Jack Sprat could eat no fat,

His wife could eat no lean.

And so between them both, you see,

They licked the platter clean.

SUGGESTION: This poem tells a story. Have children produce a short retelling or prose version of the story and place it beside the rhyming version. You can also compare the words *lean* and *clean*, helping children notice the consonant cluster.

Jack-in-the-box

Jack-in-the-box,

All shut up tight,

Not a breath of air,

Not a ray of light.

How tired he must be

Down in a heap,

We'll open the lid

And up he will leap.

SUGGESTION: Have children begin saying the verse while they are sitting down and jump up on the final line. You may want to talk with them about what a jack-in-the-box is. Ask them to imagine being scrunched up inside a box.

fold
here

137

Johnny Appleseed

Oh, the earth is good to me,

And so I thank the earth,

For giving me the things I need:

The sun, the rain, and the apple seed.

The earth is good to me.

SUGGESTION: Children may enjoy hearing the story of Johnny Appleseed who traveled all his life planting apple trees. They can also talk about how the sun and rain help the tiny seeds grow into trees.

Knock, Knock

"Knock, knock!"

"Who's there?"

"Goat."

"Goat who?"

"Goat to the door and find out."

SUGGESTION: Children enjoy "knock, knock" jokes of all kinds. Have them perform this one in the traditional question-and-answer form. You can talk about how the fact that words are run together when we talk makes this joke funny. They can practice their "delivery" with a partner and then tell the joke to family members.

fold
here

139

Ladies and Gentlemen

Ladies and gentlemen,

Come to supper—

Hot boiled beans

And very good butter.

SUGGESTION: Children can talk about their favorite foods to have for supper (or they may call it dinner) and substitute them in the poem. This poem does not rhyme, so the only consideration will be to match the number of syllables in the line. Trying words to see if they "sound right" will require children to say words and listen to syllables.

The Lady and the Crocodile

She sailed away on a bright and sunny day,

On the back of a crocodile.

"You see," said she, "he's as tame as he can be;

I'll ride him down the Nile."

The croc winked his eye as she bade them all good-bye,

Wearing a happy smile.

At the end of the ride the lady was inside,

And the smile was on the crocodile!

SUGGESTION: As children become familiar with this rhyme, it can be fun to present it with "Crocodile" (also in this volume). Children can break into two groups, each learning one of the poems. After they add pantomime movements, they can perform for the other group. Ask children to retell the story, emphasizing that it's funny because no one would ever think of riding a crocodile.

fold
here

141

The Lady With the Alligator Purse

Miss Lucy had a baby,
She named him Tiny Tim.
She put him in the bathtub
To see if he could swim.

He drank up all the water,
He ate up all the soap,
He tried to eat the bathtub,
But it wouldn't go down his throat.

Miss Lucy called the doctor,
Miss Lucy called the nurse,
Miss Lucy called the lady
With the alligator purse.

In walked the doctor,
In walked the nurse,
In walked the lady
With the alligator purse.

continued

SUGGESTION: This is a very rhythmic verse, and children can emphasize the rhyming words by clapping when they say them. Children also love to take turns acting out this poem while the rest of the group forms a circle and chants the words.

"Measles," said the doctor,
"Chicken pox," said the nurse,
"Mumps," said the lady
With the alligator purse.

"Penicillin," said the doctor,
"Aspirin," said the nurse,
"Pizza," said the lady
With the alligator purse.

A dime for the doctor,
A nickel for the nurse,
Nothing for the lady
With the alligator purse.

Out walked the doctor,
Out walked the nurse,
Out walked the lady
With the alligator purse.

Lavender's Blue

Lavender's blue,

Dilly, dilly,

Lavender's green.

When I am King,

Dilly, dilly,

You shall be Queen.

Who told you so,

Dilly, dilly,

Who told you so?

'Twas my own heart,

Dilly, dilly,

That told me so.

SUGGESTION: This is an old nonsense song. (It's included on John Langstaff's CD "Jackfish and More Songs for Singing Children.") Make an illustrated poetry chart with your students, or use tagboard strips and a pocket chart to build the poem together. Assign a small group to read or sing *Dilly, dilly*. Create two-syllable substitutes for *dilly, dilly—ducky, ducky*, for example.

The Lion and the Unicorn

The Lion and the Unicorn

Were fighting for the crown,

The Lion beat the Unicorn,

All around the town.

Some gave them white bread,

Some gave them brown,

Some gave them plum-cake,

And sent them out of town.

SUGGESTION: You may want to check on children's knowledge of the animals *lion* and *unicorn*, but they can enjoy this rhyme without knowing a great deal or can even substitute other animals' names. After they know the poem, they could say and look at the words *crown*, *town*, and *brown* as examples of rhyming words.

Listen to the Tree Bear

Listen to the tree bear

Crying in the night

Crying for his mamma

In the pale moonlight.

What will his mamma do

When she hears him cry?

She'll tuck him in a cocoa-pod

And sing a lullaby.

SUGGESTION: After children are familiar with the words of this poem, work with them on emphasizing the strong natural rhythm as they practice reciting or performing. Encourage them to change their inflection as they follow the cadence.

Little Betty Blue

Little Betty Blue

Lost her holiday shoe.

What will little Betty do?

Why, give her another

To match the other,

And then she can walk out in two.

SUGGESTION: Divide the poem into two parts of three lines each. Have groups of children take turns reciting each half. Invite children to substitute names and come up with other lost items that come in pairs—*sock, glove, earmuff, earring*. Change Betty's last name to make them rhyme.

Little Bird

Once I saw a little bird

Come hop, hop, hop;

So I cried, "Little bird,

Will you stop, stop, stop?"

I was going to the window

To say, "How do you do?"

But he shook his little tail,

And far away he flew.

SUGGESTION: You can assign one child to read the material in quotation marks expressively while others say the rest. This is a good poem to point out the function of quotation marks. Another idea is to have children substitute words for *cried* to increase their awareness of possibilities, for example, *said, shouted, called,* or *whispered.*

Little Blue Ben

Little blue Ben, who lives in the glen,

Keeps a blue cat and one blue hen

Who lays blue eggs a score and ten.

Were shall I find my little blue Ben?

SUGGESTION: You may need to explain to children that *a score and ten* actually means a number (*score* = 20). The hen lays a lot of eggs! They can change the colors to innovate on the poem. Once they are familiar with the poem, it will be easy for them to identify the rhyming words with the phonogram *-en*.

fold
here

Little Bo-Peep

Little Bo-Peep has lost her sheep,

And can't tell where to find them;

Leave them alone, and they'll come home,

Wagging their tails behind them.

Little Bo-Peep fell fast asleep

And dreamed she heard them bleating;

But when she woke, it was all a joke,

For they were still a-fleeting.

Then up she took her little crook,

And vowed that she would find them;

What was her joy to see them there,

Wagging their tails behind them.

SUGGESTION: This traditional rhyme lends itself to creating a three-page class book (one verse on each page) or individual books that children illustrate. You may want to explain that a shepherd's crook is a long stick with a hooked end that she could use to pull sheep into line and also that a *vow* is a *promise*.

Little Boy Blue

Little Boy Blue,

Come blow your horn.

The sheep's in the meadow,

The cow's in the corn.

Where is the boy

Who looks after the sheep?

He's under the haystack

Fast asleep.

Will you wake him?

No, not I,

For if I do,

He's sure to cry.

SUGGESTION: Children could get in groups and take turns reciting every other line. This story poem has many details that will be made clear if children draw the scene. Pair this with Iona Opie and Rosemary Wells's picture book *Little Boy Blue*.

fold here

151

The Little Green Frog

Glack, gloon, went the little green frog one day.

Glack, gloon, went the little green frog.

Glack, gloon, went the little green frog one day.

And his eyes went glock, glack, gloon.

SUGGESTION: Substitute other noises for the frog to make. On the last line, have children make a circle with their fingers around their eyes and stick out their tongues.

Little Mousie

See the little mousie

Creeping up the stair,

Looking for a warm nest.

There—oh, there!

SUGGESTION: After children know the words to this poem, have them add actions to make it a finger rhyme—using two fingers to *creep* up their arm and find a *warm nest* in the crook of their arm. To create additional verses, substitute two-syllable animal names, such as *sparrow* or *gerbil*.

fold
here

Little Nancy Etticoat

Little Nancy Etticoat

With a white petticoat,

And a red nose;

She has no feet or hands,

The longer she stands,

The shorter she grows.

SUGGESTION: This poem is really a riddle. What is Little Nancy Etticoat? She's a candle!

Little Peter Rabbit

Little Peter Rabbit had a fly upon his nose.

Little Peter Rabbit had a fly upon his nose.

Little Peter Rabbit had a fly upon his nose.

And he swished it and he swashed it,

And the fly flew away.

SUGGESTION: Add some rhythm instruments underneath the reciting of this poem, or invite a few children to say *swish swash* continuously while the others read the verse. You can sing it to the tune of "The Battle Hymn of the Republic."

fold here

155

The Little Plant

by Kate L. Brown

In the heart of a seed,

Buried deep, so deep,

A dear little plant

Lay fast asleep.

"Wake!" said the sunshine,

"And creep to the light."

"Wake!" said the voice

Of the raindrops bright.

The little plant heard,

And it rose to see

What the wonderful

Outside world might be.

SUGGESTION: Have the class narrate the poem, one child playing the sunshine and another the raindrops. Several children can scrunch down like seeds and slowly "grow" to stretch as high as they can.

Little Pup, Little Pup

Little pup, little pup,
What do you say?
"Woof, woof, woof!
Let's go and play."

Kitty cat, kitty cat,
How about you?
"Meow, meow, meow!
And I purr, too."

Pretty bird, pretty bird,
Have you a song?
"Tweet, tweet, tweet!
The whole day long."

Jersey cow, jersey cow,
What do you do?
"Moo, moo, moo!
And give milk, too."

Little lamb, little lamb,
What do you say?
"Baa, baa, baa!
Can Mary play?"

SUGGESTION: Once children know this poem, they will enjoy playing this game: One child recites the rhymed question and chooses a classmate to answer it. This person chooses someone to ask the next question. Ten children can play the game each time. Or, add *s* to all the animal names and have small groups of children be the animals and answer in chorus.

Little Raindrops

by Jane E. Browne

Oh, where do you come from,

You little drops of rain,

Pitter patter, pitter patter,

Down the windowpane?

They won't let me walk,

And they won't let me play,

And they won't let me go

Out of doors at all today.

ADDITIONAL VERSES:

Tell me, little raindrops,	They say I'm very naughty,	The little raindrops cannot speak,
Is that the way you play,	I have nothing else to do,	But "pitter, pitter, pat"
Pitter patter, pitter patter,	But sit here at the window,	Means "We can play on this side,
All the rainy day?	I would like to play with you.	Why can't you play on that?"

SUGGESTION: Invite children to talk about rain and how it feels. They can also say the words *pitter patter* and talk about how these words were included in the poem because they are intended to sound like rain. It might be nice to place a small version of this poem on a window of the classroom, especially on a rainy day.

Little Robin Redbreast

Little robin redbreast,

Sat upon a rail.

Niddle-noodle went his head,

Wibble-wobble went his tail.

ACTIONS:
Little robin redbreast,
Sat upon a rail. [*hold up thumb and little finger and curl down rest of fingers*]
Niddle-nooodle went his head, [*wiggle thumb*]
Wibble-wobble went his tail. [*wiggle little finger*]

SUGGESTION: This poem is full of imagery. If there is an opportunity, have children observe birds that are perched on trees or telephone lines. This poem is a good one to place near a window. Children can also illustrate it with pictures of robins.

Little Sally Waters

Little Sally Waters, sitting in the sun,

Crying and weeping, lonesome little one.

Rise, Sally, rise;

Wipe off your eyes;

Fly to the east, Sally, fly to the west,

Fly to the one you like the very best.

SUGGESTION: Assign someone to play Sally [or Wally]. This child sits in the center of the circle and acts out the words, crying and weeping as the other children sing. On cue, Sally [Wally] rises, flies to the east and flies to the west. The player she goes to on the last line becomes the next Sally [Wally], and the game goes on until everyone has had a turn.

Little Silver Airplane

Little silver airplane

Up in the sky,

Where are you going to

Flying so high?

Over the mountains

Over the sea

Little silver airplane

Please take me.

SUGGESTION: Children can talk about seeing planes in the air and wondering where they are going and/or actually flying in a plane.

Little White Rabbit

Little white rabbit,

Hop on one foot, one foot.

Little white rabbit,

Hop on two feet, two feet.

Little white rabbit,

Hop on three feet, three feet.

Little white rabbit,

Hop on four feet, four feet.

Little white rabbit,

Hop, hop, hop, hop, hop, hop.

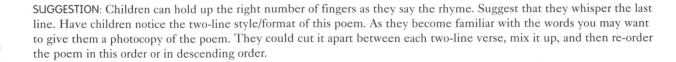

SUGGESTION: Children can hold up the right number of fingers as they say the rhyme. Suggest that they whisper the last line. Have children notice the two-line style/format of this poem. As they become familiar with the words you may want to give them a photocopy of the poem. They could cut it apart between each two-line verse, mix it up, and then re-order the poem in this order or in descending order.

London Bridge

London Bridge is falling down,
Falling down, falling down,
London Bridge is falling down,
My fair lady.

Build it up with iron bars,
Iron bars, iron bars,
Build it up with iron bars,
My fair lady.

Iron bars will bend and break,
Bend and break, bend and break,
Iron bars will bend and break,
My fair lady.

ADDITIONAL VERSES:

Build it up with pins and needles,
Pins and needles, pins and needles,
Build it up with pins and needles,
My fair lady.

Pins and needles rust and bend,
Rust and bend, rust and bend,
Pins and needles rust and bend,
My fair lady.

Build it up with gravel and stone,
Gravel and stone, gravel and stone,
Build it up with gravel and stone,
My fair lady.

Gravel and stone will wash away,
Wash away, wash away,
Gravel and stone will wash away,
My fair lady.

SUGGESTION: Have children suggest other materials to use to rebuild the bridge: gold and silver, pirate treasure, and so on. Play a game in which two children form London Bridge by joining hands, arms stretched upward. Ask the other children to march under the arch in single file as they sing the song. On *My fair lady* the arch falls, capturing a child, who becomes an observer. Continue until all children have been caught.

Looby-loo

Here we dance, looby-loo,

Here we dance, looby-light,

Here we dance, looby-loo,

All on a Saturday night.

I put my right hand in,

I put my right hand out,

I give my hand a shake, shake, shake,

And turn myself about. Oh,

Here we dance, looby-loo,

Here we dance, looby-light,

Here we dance, looby-loo,

All on a Saturday night.

SUGGESTION: Use the song to play a game: have children join hands and skip in a circle in the direction you indicate, stop and enact the motions described in the second verse, and then skip around in the opposite direction. Let children invent their own actions for the second verse: *left hand in*, *right foot in*, *left elbow in*, and so forth.

The Man in the Moon

The man in the moon

Looked out of the moon,

His sides they shook with mirth.

"It's time for all

Children to crawl

Into their beds on Earth."

VARIATION:
The man in the moon
Came down too soon,
And asked his way to Norwich;
He went by the south
And burned his mouth
While supping on plum porridge.

SUGGESTION: You may want to explain that *shook with mirth* means *laughing*. Children can laugh and feel their sides shaking with mirth. Children are sometimes curious about words such as *porridge*, which can be explained as similar to oatmeal. Ask them to think what *supping* might mean; they will connect it to *supper*.

Mary Ann, Mary Ann

Mary Ann, Mary Ann,

Make the porridge in a pan.

Make it thick, make it thin,

Make it any way you can.

SUGGESTION: Substitute different names that include Ann such as *Betty Ann, Peggy Ann,* or *Carol Ann;* invite the children to guess what *porridge* is. As children practice, they can recite the verse faster and faster.

Mary Had a Little Lamb

Mary had a little lamb,
Little lamb, little lamb,
Mary had a little lamb,
Its fleece was white as snow.

It followed her to school one day,
School one day, school one day,
It followed her to school one day,
Which was against the rule.

It made the children laugh and play,
Laugh and play, laugh and play,
It made the children laugh and play
To see a lamb at school.

ADDITIONAL VERSES:
And so the teacher turned it out,
Turned it out, turned it out,
And so the teacher turned it out,
But still it lingered near.

What makes the lamb love Mary so,
Mary so, Mary so?
What makes the lamb love Mary so?
The eager children cry.

Why, Mary loves the lamb, you know,
Lamb, you know, lamb, you know,
Why, Mary loves the lamb, you know,
The teacher did reply.

SUGGESTION: The image of a little lamb following a child to school is an enjoyable one for children. Teach the children to sing the rhyme. Link this poem with Sara Hale's picture book *Mary Had a Little Lamb*, photoillustrated by Bruce McMillan (this will be especially helpful for English-language learners).

Mary Wore Her Red Dress

Mary wore her red dress, red dress, red dress.
Mary wore her red dress
All day long.

Mary wore her red hat, red hat, red hat.
Mary wore her red hat
All day long.

Mary wore her red shoes, red shoes, red shoes.
Mary wore her red shoes
All day long.

Mary wore her red gloves, red gloves, red gloves.
Mary wore her red gloves
All day long.

Mary was a red bird, red bird, red bird.
Mary was a red bird
All day long!

SUGGESTION: This is an old Texas folksong. Eliminate the last verse and make it a poem about different children wearing different-color clothes. Children enjoy substituting their own names and color choices. You may want to pair it with the story of Kate Bear's birthday party in Merle Peek's picture book *Mary Wore Her Red Dress and Henry Wore His Green Sneakers*.

Mary's Canary

Mary had a pretty bird,

Feather's bright and yellow,

Slender legs—upon my word

He was a pretty fellow.

The sweetest note he always sung,

Which much delighted Mary.

She often, where the cage was hung,

Sat hearing her canary.

SUGGESTION: Ask two children to act out or pantomime this verse as the class recites it together. As an alternative, consider dividing the class and allowing one group to become audible "canaries" as background for the second verse. And then repeat giving the other group a chance to do their birdcalls. This is also a fun poem to revisit when children are working to recognize rhymes and/or identifying one-, two-, and three-syllable words.

fold here

169

Merrily We Roll Along

Merrily we roll along,

Roll along, roll along.

Merrily we roll along,

O'er the deep blue sea.

SUGGESTION: Invite the children to say the rhyme in unison or as a round. Explain that *o'er* is a contraction for *over* that people sometimes use in poems. When you have finished reading the poem, invite the children to name all the ways they might roll across the sea: canoe, sail boat, submarine, kayak, speed boat. And what other ways might they move across the sea? Paddle, sail, glide, zoom, zip . . .

Mistress Mary

Mistress Mary, quite contrary,

How does your garden grow?

With silver bells and cockleshells,

And pretty maids all in a row.

SUGGESTION: Divide the class in two; half can ask the question, and the other half responds. Explain that *silver bells* and *cockleshells* are types of flowers.

fold
here

171

Monday Morning

This is the way we wash our clothes,

Wash our clothes, wash our clothes,

This is the way we wash our clothes

All on a Monday morning.

This is the way we hang them up,

Hang them up, hang them up,

This is the way we hang them up

All on a Monday morning.

This is the way we fold our clothes,

Fold our clothes, fold our clothes,

This is the way we fold our clothes

All on a Monday morning.

SUGGESTION: Create new *This is the way* verses with the same structure. Substitute the names of other days of the week.

Moon, Moon

Moon, moon,

Silvery spoon,

Floating still

On a night in June.

Moon, moon,

Back too soon,

White and pale

In the afternoon.

SUGGESTION: Ask children if they have ever seen the moon in the sky during the day. They can discuss the many different ways the moon looks.

fold here

173

The Moon Shines Bright

The moon shines bright,

The stars give a light.

You may play at any game

At ten o'clock at night.

SUGGESTION: Use this poem right before summer vacation. Children may remember how the days are very long and that moonlight and starlight seem almost like day. Prompt them to remember this poem as they are playing late.

The More We Get Together

Oh, the more we get together,

Together, together,

Oh, the more we get together,

The happier we'll be.

For your friends are my friends,

And my friends are your friends.

Oh, the more we get together,

The happier we'll be!

SUGGESTION: The repetition in this song will make it enjoyable to sing. It may be interesting for children to examine the first two sentences of the second verse. They can discuss how they sound almost alike and have the same words but the meaning is slightly changed.

fold here

175

Mouse in a Hole

A mouse lived in a little hole,

Lived quietly in a little hole.

When all was quiet, as quiet as can be . . .

OUT POPPED HE!

SUGGESTION: Invite the children to read the third line very softly and pop up and shout the last line.

My Apple

Look at my apple, it is nice and round.

It fell from a tree, down to the ground.

Come, let me share my apple, please do!

My mother can cut it half in two—

One half for me and one half for you.

ACTIONS:

Look at my apple, it is nice and round. [*cup hands*]

It fell from a tree, down to the ground. [*move fingers in a downward motion*]

Come, let me share my apple, please do! [*beckoning motion*]

My mother can cut it half in two— [*slicing motion*]

One half for me and one half for you. [*hold out two hands, sharing halves*]

SUGGESTION: Children can have a discussion about what *sharing* means and also what *half* means in the poem. What would they do if there were three friends? (*My mother can cut it into three—one for each of you and one for me.*)

My Aunt Jane

My Aunt Jane,

She came from France,

To teach to me the polka dance;

First the heel,

And then the toe,

That's the way

The dance should go.

SUGGESTION: Children may enjoy moving from one leg to another and, while standing on one leg, tapping heel and toe of the other. This will make a kind of dance that will provide some good, quick exercise.

My Big Balloon

I can make a big balloon,

Watch me while I blow.

Small at first then bigger,

Watch it grow and grow.

Do you think it's big enough?

Maybe I should stop.

For if I blow much longer,

My balloon will surely pop!

SUGGESTION: Bring in a balloon to blow up, and this poem will really come to life. Have children recite the poem and shout "pop!" on the last line. Print the words to the verse on a poetry chart for children to illustrate. Assign one child to write *POP!* on the chart in capital letters.

My Bike

One wheel, two wheels, on the ground,

My feet make the pedals go 'round and 'round.

The handlebars help me steer so straight,

Down the sidewalk and through the gate.

ACTIONS:

One wheel, two wheels, on the ground, [*make circle with arms*]

My feet make the pedals go 'round and 'round. [*lift feet and pretend to pedal bike*]

The handlebars help me steer so straight, [*pretend to steer*]

Down the sidewalk and through the gate. [*shade eyes as if looking at something in the distance*]

SUGGESTION: Have children act out the poem as shown above. Give them a reproduced copy of the rhyme. They can illustrate it with a bike, choosing the color and decorations they like.

My Bonnie Lies Over the Ocean

My Bonnie lies over the ocean,
My Bonnie lies over the sea.
My Bonnie lies over the ocean,
Please bring back my Bonnie to me.

Chorus:
    Bring back, bring back,
    Oh, bring back my Bonnie to me, to me.
    Bring back, bring back,
    Oh, bring back my Bonnie to me.

Oh, blow ye winds over the ocean,
And blow ye winds over the sea.
Oh, blow ye winds over the ocean,
And bring back my Bonnie to me.

Chorus

The winds have blown over the ocean,
The winds have blown over the sea.
The winds have blown over the ocean,
And brought back my Bonnie to me.

Chorus

SUGGESTION: Children may want to talk about *Bonnie* as a girl's name, but have them learn that it also means *pretty* and might be something to call someone you like—a girl or a boy. (Originally the song was about "Bonny Prince Charlie.")

My Favorite Toys

I have a lot of favorite toys.
I cannot choose just one.
I need to keep them all around
For different kinds of fun.

A book, a doll,
A drum, a ball,
And, of course, my teddy bear.
A wagon, a bike,
And finally I like
The jack-in-the-box sitting there.

As you can see, I need them all
For work and play and rest.
When you go home to find your toys,
Which ones do you like best?

SUGGESTION: Use interactive writing to make a chart or class book about toys. ("Rayshawn's favorite toy is _____.") They will be adding more modern toys to the list. Each child can make an illustration to glue on the chart or in the book.

My Hat, It Has Three Corners

My hat, it has three corners,

Three corners has my hat;

And had it not three corners,

It would not be my hat.

ACTIONS:
My hat, it has three corners [*point to self*]
Three corners has my hat; [*point to head*]
And had it not three corners, [*hold up three fingers*]
It would not be my hat. [*bend arm and point to elbow*]

SUGGESTION: After children are familiar with the poem, put it in a pocket chart with individual words on cards (or write it on chart paper). On each repetition, eliminate a word, but use the action in silence each time that word would have been said. Children will find the last verses (mostly gestures) funny.

My Love for You

I know you little,

I love you lots;

My love for you

Would fill ten pots,

Fifteen buckets,

Sixteen cans,

Three teacups,

And four dishpans.

SUGGESTION: Substitute other number words or objects to create new verses of this poem.

Night, Knight

"Night, night,"

Said one knight

To the other knight

The other night.

"Night, night, Knight."

SUGGESTION: Children may know what a *knight* is from games or television. If not, explain the word *knight* and invite children to compare it with *night*. They can talk about what makes the tongue twister funny.

fold
here

185

Nut Tree

I had a little nut tree,

Nothing would it bear,

But a silver nutmeg

And a golden pear.

The king of Spain's daughter

Came to visit me,

And all for the sake

Of my little nut tree.

I skipped over water,

I danced over sea,

And all the birds

Couldn't catch me.

SUGGESTION: Teach children this nursery song—there are recorded versions on many CDs and audiocassettes, and the music enhances the words. The images of the *silver nutmeg* and the *golden pear* are magical.

Oats, Peas, Beans

Oats, peas, beans, and barley grow,

Oats, peas, beans, and barley grow,

Do you or I or anyone know

How oats, peas, beans, and barley grow?

First the farmer sows his seeds,

Then he stands and takes his ease,

Stamps his feet, and claps his hands,

And turns around to view the land.

Waiting for a partner,

Waiting for a partner,

Open the ring and take one in,

And then we'll dance and gaily sing.

SUGGESTION: Have one child play the part of the farmer and stand in the center of a circle. Children join hands and skip left as they sing. The "farmer" acts out the second verse and then chooses a partner during the third verse while the class continues to skip around. Then the partner or another child becomes the "farmer," and the song is repeated. John Langstaff's CD *Songs for Singing Children* includes a great rendition of this old song.

fold here

187

Old Dan Tucker

Old Dan Tucker went to town

Riding a goat and leading a hound.

The hound gave a yelp and the goat gave a jump

And old Dan Tucker landed on a stump.

SUGGESTION: Children can talk about what riding a goat would be like and why it would be so hard to do. After they know the poem, they could quickly locate words that end with *mp*.

The Old Gray Cat

The old gray cat is sleeping, sleeping, sleeping,

The old gray cat is sleeping in the house.

The little mice are creeping, creeping, creeping,

The little mice are creeping through the house.

The old gray cat is waking, waking, waking,

The old gray cat is waking in the house.

The old gray cat is chasing, chasing, chasing,

The old gray cat is chasing through the house.

All the mice are squealing, squealing, squealing,

All the mice are squealing through the house.

SUGGESTION: This song is fun for children to act out. It also is a good base for a five-page book that they can illustrate and use for shared reading. You can use it to have children locate words with *ing* at the end. Point out the different uses of *in* and *through*.

Old King Cole

Old King Cole was a merry old soul,

And a merry old soul was he;

He called for his pipe, and he called for his bowl,

And he called for his fiddlers three.

Every fiddler had a fiddle,

And a very fine fiddle had he;

Tweedle-dee, tweedle-dee, went the fiddlers three,

And merry we will be.

SUGGESTION: This traditional rhyme is fun to say, especially when accompanied by rhythm sticks or other musical instruments.

Old MacDonald Had a Farm

Old MacDonald had a farm, E – I – E – I – O!

And on his farm he had a dog, E – I – E – I – O!

With a bow-wow here, and a bow-wow there,

Here a bow, there a wow, everywhere a bow-wow,

Old MacDonald had a farm, E – I – E – I – O!

And on his farm he had some ducks, E – I – E – I – O!

With a quack-quack here, and a quack-quack there,

Here a quack, there a quack, everywhere a quack-quack,

Old MacDonald had a farm, E – I – E – I – O!

ADDITIONAL VERSES:
chicks—chick-chick
cows—moo-moo
pigs—oink-oink
horses—neigh-neigh
cats—meow-meow

SUGGESTION: Teach the song, and then see if children wish to choose their own animals and the noises they make. Motions may be created for each animal. This song can be cumulative, repeating all animal noises each time a new one is added. Also read the book *Ms. MacDonald Has a Class* by Jan Ormerod.

The Old Man and the Cow

by Edward Lear

There was an old man who said, "How

Shall I flee from this horrible cow?

I will sit on this stile,

And continue to smile,

Which may soften the heart of that cow."

SUGGESTION: Help the children notice the rhyming pattern by having them whisper or shout the rhyming words. Children may be curious about a *stile*, which is a set of steps up and over a fence.

Old Mother Hubbard

Old Mother Hubbard went to the cupboard
To give her poor dog a bone.

But when she got there, the cupboard was bare,
And so the poor dog had none.

She went to the hatter's to buy him a hat.
When she came back, he was feeding the cat.

She went to the barber's to buy him a wig.
When she came back, he was dancing a jig.

She went to the tailor's to buy him a coat.
When she came back, he was riding a goat.

She went to the cobbler's to buy him some shoes.
When she came back, he was reading the news.

SUGGESTION: This is a great story poem about a dog whose owner, Mother Hubbard, goes out to buy him things. Create new verses with the same pattern. (*She went to the cleaner's to get him some clothes.* / *When she came back, he was licking his toes.*) Make a cupboard that opens and have children draw and label the contents.

The Old Woman

The old woman must stand at the tub, tub, tub,

The dirty clothes to rub, rub, rub.

But when they are clean and fit to be seen,

She'll dress like a lady and dance on the green.

SUGGESTION: Ask children what they think the *green* might be (grassy area, park, a place where people gather to meet, talk, or dance).

On Saturday Night

On Saturday night I lost my wife,

And where do you think I found her?

Up in the moon, singing a tune,

And all the stars around her.

On Top of Spaghetti

On top of spaghetti,

All covered with cheese,

I lost my last meatball,

When somebody sneezed.

It rolled off the table

And onto the floor

And then my poor meatball

Rolled out of the door.

So, if you eat spaghetti,

All covered with cheese,

Hold on to your meatballs,

And don't ever sneeze.

SUGGESTION: Children will love singing this nonsense song to the tune of "On Top of Old Smokey."

One Finger, One Thumb, Keep Moving

One finger, one thumb, keep moving,

One finger, one thumb, keep moving,

One finger, one thumb, keep moving,

We'll all be merry and bright.

One finger, one thumb, one arm, keep moving,

One finger, one thumb, one arm, keep moving,

One finger, one thumb, one arm, keep moving,

We'll all be merry and bright.

One finger, one thumb, one arm, one leg, keep moving,

One finger, one thumb, one arm, one leg, keep moving,

One finger, one thumb, one arm, one leg, keep moving,

We'll all be merry and bright.

ADDITIONAL VERSES:

One finger, one thumb, one arm, one leg, one nod of the head, keep moving . . . .

One finger, one thumb, one arm, one leg, one nod of the head, stand up, sit down, keep moving . . .

One finger, one thumb, one arm, one leg, one nod of the head, stand up, sit down, turn around, keep moving . . .

SUGGESTION: This poem gives children a chance to move around and stretch as they say the words and perform the actions, adding one additional body part with each new verse.

One for the Money

One for the money,

Two for the show,

Three to make ready,

And four to go!

SUGGESTION: Children can hold up the right number of fingers for the lines of the poem. It also is fun to use as children are getting ready to leave at the end of the day.

One for Sorrow

One for sorrow,

Two for joy,

Three for a girl,

Four for a boy,

Five for silver,

Six for gold,

Seven for a secret

Never to be told.

SUGGESTION: Have the children hold up the correct number of fingers on each line. Create new verses with the same structure.

One Man Went to Mow

One man went to mow,

Went to mow a meadow.

One man and his dog

Went to mow a meadow.

Two men went to mow,

Went to mow a meadow.

Two men, one man and his dog

Went to mow a meadow.

Three men went to mow,

Went to mow a meadow.

Three men, two men, one man and his dog

Went to mow a meadow.

SUGGESTION: How do you mow a meadow? City children and English-language learners may need to see a picture of a meadow to help make the concept clear. Continue the rhyme to ten, increasing the number of men with each stanza.

One Misty, Moisty Morning

One misty, moisty morning

When cloudy was the weather,

There I met an old man

Clothed all in leather.

He began to compliment

And I began to grin,

"How do you do?"

And "How do you do?"

And "How do you do?" again!

SUGGESTION: The *s* sounds in the first line set a damp, foggy mood. Pairs of children can act out the rhyme—one the child, one the old man—by taking off their imaginary hats, bowing, and saying, *How do you do?*

fold
here

201

One, Two, How Do You Do?

One, two,
How do?
One, two, three,
Clap with me.
One, two, three, four,
Jump on the floor.
One, two, three, four, five,
Look bright and alive.
One, two, three, four, five, six,
Your shoe we'll have to fix.
One, two, three, four, five, six, seven,
Can we make it to eleven?
One, two, three, four, five, six, seven, eight,
Draw a circle on a big round plate.
One, two, three, four, five, six, seven, eight, nine,
Get ready, it's time to stand in line.
One, two, three, four, five, six, seven, eight, nine, ten,
Let's go back and start all over again.

SUGGESTION: Children enjoy acting this one out; it's especially fun to do with a partner.

One, Two, Three, Four, Five

One, two, three, four, five,

Once I caught a fish alive.

Six, seven, eight, nine, ten,

Then I let him go again.

Why did you let him go?

Because he bit my finger so.

Which finger did he bite?

This little finger on the right.

SUGGESTION: This is an easy poem to learn and chant. Adding motions increases the fun and helps children remember the words.

Out

Out goes the rat,

Out goes the cat,

Out goes the lady

With the big green hat.

Y – O – U spells you,

O – U – T spells out!

SUGGESTION: This verse may be recited as a jump-rope rhyme. It can also be used to accompany a counting-out circle game: the child in the center points to ten students, one at a time, while saying *Y–O–U spells you, O–U–T spells out!*; then the child who is *out* goes to the center and counts someone else out.

Over in the Meadow

Over in the meadow, in the sand, in the sun,

Lived an old mother frog and her little froggy one.

"Croak!" said the mother, "I croak," said the one,

So they croaked and they croaked in the sand, in the sun.

Over in the meadow, in the stream so blue,

Lived an old mother fish and her little fishies two.

"Swim!" said the mother, "We swim," said the two,

So they swam and they swam in the stream so blue.

Over in the meadow, on a branch of the tree,

Lived an old mother bird and her little birdies three.

"Sing!" said the mother, "We sing," said the three,

So they sang and they sang on a branch of the tree.

SUGGESTION: Invite children to create additional verses (even if they are not able to maintain the rhyme scheme) centered on other animals, their habitats, and their typical sounds and actions. Invite your English-language learners to share the names of animals in their native language.

Papa's Glasses

These are Papa's glasses.

This is Papa's hat.

This is how he folds his hands

And puts them in his lap.

ACTIONS:
These are Papa's glasses. [*make glasses with fingers*]
This is Papa's hat. [*tap head*]
This is how he folds his hands [*fold hands*]
And puts them in his lap. [*place hands in lap*]

SUGGESTION: Have the children complete the actions along with the rhyme. Create new verses about Nana's or Grandma's glasses. You can also substitute children's names for *Papa* and have one child act out the poem while others say it.

Peanut Butter and Jelly

First you take the peanuts,

And you dig 'em, you dig 'em,

Dig 'em, dig 'em, dig 'em.

Then you crush 'em, you crush 'em,

Crush 'em, crush 'em, crush 'em.

Then you spread 'em, you spread 'em,

Spread 'em, spread 'em, spread 'em.

For your peanut, peanut butter and jelly,

Peanut, peanut butter and jelly.

ADDITIONAL VERSES:

Then you take the berries,
And you pick 'em, you pick 'em,
Pick 'em, pick 'em, pick 'em.
Then you smash 'em, you smash 'em,
Smash 'em, smash 'em, smash 'em.
Then you smooth 'em, you smooth 'em,
Smooth 'em, smooth 'em, smooth 'em.

For your peanut, peanut butter and jelly,
Peanut, peanut butter and jelly.

Then you take the sandwich,
And you bite it, you bite it,
Bite it, bite it, bite it.
Then you chew it, you chew it,
Chew it, chew it, chew it.
Then you swallow it, you swallow it,
Swallow it, swallow it, swallow it.

'Cause it's peanut, peanut butter and jelly,
Peanut, peanut butter and jelly.

SUGGESTION: There are several different versions of this popular rhyme and you may want to compare them. If you are working with a written version, children may be curious about the use of apostrophes in *'em* and *'cause*. This is a good way to help them understand that apostrophes sometimes stand for letters that have been left out of words.

Pease Porridge Hot

Pease porridge hot,

Pease porridge cold,

Pease porridge in the pot,

Nine days old.

Some like it hot,

Some like it cold,

Some like it in the pot,

Nine days old.

SUGGESTION: Have children clap while saying this particular rhyme. They will enjoy the alliteration with the beginning sound and letter of *p*. They can locate words that begin with *p*.

Peter Piper

Peter Piper picked a peck of pickled peppers;

A peck of pickled peppers Peter Piper picked.

If Peter Piper picked a peck of pickled peppers,

Where's the peck of pickled peppers Peter Piper

picked?

SUGGESTION: This tongue twister can be read and recited slowly at first and then faster and faster. Children might need help with the concept of a *peck* of pickled peppers. Ask your group what foods and other staples their families buy in large quantities.

Polly, Put the Kettle On

Polly, put the kettle on,

Polly, put the kettle on,

Polly, put the kettle on,

We'll all have tea.

Sukey, take it off again,

Sukey, take it off again,

Sukey, take it off again,

They've all gone home.

SUGGESTION: Have the children sing or chant the text with a partner, clapping each other's palms and then their own to the beat. Let them substitute their own names.

Polly Wolly Doodle

Oh, I went down South
For to see my Sal
Sing Polly wolly doodle all the day
My Sal, she is
A spunky gal
Sing Polly wolly doodle all the day

Chorus:
> Fare thee well, fare thee well
> Fare thee well my fairy fay
> For I'm going to Lou'siana
> For to see my Susyanna
> Sing Polly wolly doodle all the day

ADDITIONAL VERSES:

Behind the barn,
Down on my knees
Sing Polly wolly doodle all the day
I thought I heard
A chicken sneeze
Sing Polly wolly doodle all the day

Chorus

He sneezed so hard
With the whooping cough
Sing Polly wolly doodle all the day
He sneezed his head
And the tail right off
Sing Polly wolly doodle all the day

Chorus

Oh, a grasshopper sittin'
On a railroad track
Sing Polly wolly doodle all the day
A-pickin' his teeth
With a carpet tack
Sing Polly wolly doodle all the day.

Chorus

Oh, I went to bed
But it wasn't any use
Sing Polly wolly doodle all the day
My feet stuck out
Like a chicken roost
Sing Polly wolly doodle all the day

Chorus

SUGGESTION: Children will enjoy singing this traditional song. As they learn verses, look at the funny aspects of the song. Use judgment about how many verses to teach children at once, but you can continue to add verses throughout the year as they learn the song.

Pop! Goes the Weasel

All around the mulberry bush,

The monkey chased the weasel,

The monkey thought t'was all in fun,

Pop! goes the weasel.

A penny for a spool of thread,

A penny for a needle,

That's the way the money goes,

Pop! goes the weasel.

Rufus has the whooping cough,

Poor Sally has the measles,

That's the way the doctor goes,

Pop! goes the weasel.

SUGGESTION: Children will enjoy reciting or singing the words and jumping up to shout *Pop!* Some children may need an explanation of the word *weasel*. Playing a recording of a sung version is always enjoyable, or children could play the tune on homemade kazoos (tape or rubber-band a square of waxed paper around one end of a paper tube, and have children place the mouth over the other end of the tube and hum).

Pumpkin Orange

We had a pumpkin orange.

We gave it two big eyes.

We cut around a tiny nose

A funny mouth that smiles.

Now we'll hide behind the hedge

And wait until it's dark.

Then when _____ comes along,

Up we'll jump! "Boo!" we'll shout!

What a surprise!

SUGGESTION: After the children have learned the poem, give them time to create the perfect props: orange jack-o'-lanterns, attached to tongue depressors or kraft sticks, to hold up when they shout *Boo!* For variety and suspense, insert different children's names in the poem.

The Pussycat and the Queen

"Pussycat, pussycat, where have you been?"

"I've been to London to visit the Queen!"

"Pussycat, pussycat, what did you do there?"

"I frightened a little mouse under her chair."

SUGGESTION: Read this poem as a question and answer, with half the class saying each role.

The Queen of Hearts

The Queen of Hearts
She made some tarts,
All on a summer's day.

The Knave of Hearts
He stole the tarts
And took them clean away.

The King of Hearts
Called for the tarts
Until his voice was sore.

The Knave of Hearts
Brought back the tarts
And said he'd steal no more.

SUGGESTION: Children need to know that *tarts* are little pies with no top crust, usually filled with something sweet, such as jam, custard, or fruit. They also need to know about royalty: kings, queen, knaves, and so forth. Divide the class into four groups and have each group read one stanza of the poem.

Roosters Crow

Roosters crow in the morn

To tell us to rise,

And he who lies late

Will never be wise.

For early to bed

And early to rise

Is the way to be healthy

And wealthy and wise.

SUGGESTION: Children may not know that roosters crow at dawn and that people used to depend on the sound to wake them up. Compare a rooster's crow to an alarm or clock radio. Discuss why it is important to get enough sleep.

'Round and 'Round

'Round and 'round the garden

Went the teddy bear;

One step,

Two steps,

And he's almost there.

'Round and 'round the haystack

Went the little mouse;

One step,

Two steps,

In his little house.

SUGGESTION: If your class has a teddy bear, this may be the time he gets to take a spin as a child acts out the poem. Or the whole class may mime the rhyme. This is also a good chant for lining up in preparation for leaving the classroom as a group.

Rub-a-dub-dub

Rub-a-dub-dub,
Three men in a tub,
And who do you think were there?
The butcher, the baker,
The candlestick maker,
And all had come from the fair.

Rub-a-dub-dub,
Three men in a tub,
And how do you think they got there?
They all jumped out of
A rotten potato!
'Twas enough to make a fish stare.

SUGGESTION: Have a small group of children repeat *Rub-a-dub-dub* while the rest read the rhyme.

Sam, Sam, the Butcher Man

Sam, Sam, the butcher man,

Washed his face in a frying pan,

Combed his hair with a wagon wheel,

And died with a toothache in his heel.

SUGGESTION: This nonsense verse uses funny images for humor. Substitute other names and occupations, for example: *John, John, the fireman, | Washed his hands in a pizza pan, | Combed his hair with a hunk of cheese, | And died with an earache in his knees.*

Say and Touch

Say red and touch your head.

Say sky and touch your eye.

Say bear and touch your hair.

Say hear and touch your ear.

Say south and touch your mouth.

Say rose and touch your nose.

Say in and touch your chin.

Say rest and touch your chest.

Say farm and touch your arm.

Say yummy and touch your tummy.

Say bee and touch your knee.

Say neat and touch your feet.

SUGGESTION: This poem is a little like the old game Simon Says. Children recite the rhymes as they point to the body part named—head, eye, ear, and so on. After they know the poem, the person who is "it" (the teacher at first) can say a verse that does *not* rhyme. Children should follow directions *only* on a rhyme.

She'll Be Coming 'Round the Mountain

She'll be coming 'round the mountain

When she comes, toot, toot,

She'll be coming 'round the mountain

When she comes, toot, toot,

She'll be coming 'round the mountain,

She'll be coming 'round the mountain,

She'll be coming 'round the mountain

When she comes, toot, toot.

ADDITIONAL VERSES:
She'll be driving six white horses
When she comes, whoa, back,
She'll be driving six white horses
When she comes, whoa, back,
She'll be driving six white horses,
She'll be driving six white horses,
She'll be driving six white horses
When she comes, whoa, back.

And we'll all sing "Welcome"
When she comes, oh, yes,
And we'll all sing "Welcome"
When she comes, oh, yes,
And we'll all sing "Welcome,"
Oh we'll all sing "Welcome,"
And we'll all sing "Welcome"
When she comes, oh, yes.

SUGGESTION: If you have children in your classroom who speak other languages, invite them to tell their classmates how to say *welcome* or *hello* in those languages. Ask them to teach the word or words to the class (if possible, verify the correct spellings and post the words in the classroom). Then sing the song again, replacing *Welcome* with a greeting in another language.

Shoo Fly

Shoo fly, don't bother me.

Shoo fly, don't bother me.

Shoo fly, don't bother me.

For I belong to somebody.

SUGGESTION: Extend this exuberant song by sharing Iza Trapani's picture book *Shoe Fly!* the story of an intrepid mouse who fights a persistent fly. The music and words to all the verses of the song are included on the last page of the book. Seeing the illustrations while hearing the story supports English-language learners and gives them a stimulating experience with language.

Sing a Song of Sixpence

Sing a song of sixpence,
A pocket full of rye.
Four and twenty blackbirds
Baked in a pie!

When the pie was opened,
The birds began to sing.
Wasn't that a dainty dish
To set before the king?

The king was in the counting-house,
Counting out his money.
The queen was in the parlor,
Eating bread and honey.

The maid was in the garden,
Hanging out the clothes
When down came a blackbird
And snapped off her nose!

SUGGESTION: Have the children sing the song. They can snap fingers or clap on the word *snapped*. Divide the children into four groups and each can practice one stanza to perform.

Sing, Sing

Sing, sing,

What shall I sing?

That cat's run away

With the pudding string!

Do, do,

What shall I do?

The cat's run away

With the pudding, too.

SUGGESTION: This poem *sings* with lots of *ing* words. Find them together. Create some new verses using other verbs and different animals. Children may like to know that in this verse *pudding* is a sausage (like a salami or hot dog) and does have a string.

Sippity Sup

Sippity sup, sippity sup,

Bread and milk from a china cup,

Bread and milk

From a bright silver spoon,

Made of a piece

Of the bright silver moon!

Sippity sup, sippity sup,

Sippity, sippity, sup.

SUGGESTION: Have three or four children dramatize this poem, using plastic cups and saucers and pretending to eat and drink as they recite their lines. Ask the rest of the class to provide a "munching" or "slurping" chorus or softly repeat the words *sippity sup* throughout the recitation.

fold here

225

Six Little Ducks

Six little ducks that I once knew,

Fat ducks, skinny ones, fair ones too,

But the one little duck with the feather on his back,

He led the others with his quack-quack-quack.

Down to the meadow they would go,

Wig-wag, wiggle-wag, to and fro,

But the one little duck with the feather on his back,

He led the others with his quack-quack-quack.

SUGGESTION: Children can pretend to be ducks as they sing this song. Alternatively, have six children be the ducks with the leader saying the *quack, quack, quack*.

Six Little Snowmen

Six little snowmen all made of snow,

Six little snowmen standing in a row.

Out came the sun and stayed all day,

One little snowman melted away.

Five little snowmen all made of snow.

SUGGESTION: This countdown poem begins with six and ends with zero as, one by one, the snowmen melt. Children can dramatize the snowmen melting onto the classroom floor.

Sleep, Baby, Sleep!

Sleep, baby, sleep!

Thy father watches the sheep;

Thy mother is shaking the dreamland tree,

And down falls a little dream on thee:

Sleep, baby, sleep!

Sleep, baby, sleep!

The large stars are the sheep;

The wee stars are the lambs, I guess,

The fair moon is the shepherdess:

Sleep, baby, sleep!

SUGGESTION: Talking about some of the vocabulary in the poem will help children understand the unfamiliar words, for example, *dreamland tree*, *sheep*, *lambs*, and *shepherdess*. Have children whisper the final words. Some may not know that *thy* is the same as *your* and *wee* means *little*.

Slip on Your Raincoat

Slip on your raincoat,

Pull on your galoshes;

Wading in puddles

Makes splishes and sploshes.

SUGGESTION: Compare this poem to "Little Raindrops" in this volume. How are the poems similar? How are they different? Talk about how *splishes* and *sploshes* sound like the noise you make splashing in puddles.

fold
here

Slowly, Slowly

Slowly, slowly, very slowly,

Creeps the garden snail.

Slowly, slowly, very slowly,

Up the wooden rail.

Quickly, quickly, very quickly,

Runs the little mouse.

Quickly, quickly, very quickly,

'Round about the house.

SUGGESTION: Let children create motions to go with the words of this poem. They will learn the meaning of *opposite* as they make the snail move slowly and the mouse run quickly. See if they can come up with other opposite words and movements.

The Smile Song

I've got something in my pocket

That belongs upon my face.

I keep it very close at hand

In a most convenient place.

I think you wouldn't guess it

If you guessed a long long while,

So I'll take it out and put it on.

It's a great big happy smile.

SUGGESTION: Children can pantomime holding something in a pocket during the first seven lines and then taking it out and putting it across the face, leaving a big smile. Have children sing this rhyme to the tune of "The Brownie Song."

fold
here

231

A Snail

A snail crept up the lily's stalk;

"How nice and smooth," said he;

"It's quite a pleasant evening walk,

And just the thing for me!"

SUGGESTION: Use this poem to call children's attention to quotation marks. Partners or small groups can take turns reading expressively what the snail says. You can also pair it with "Slowly, Slowly" (also in this volume) featuring another creeping snail.

Snow, Snow, Fly Away

Snow, snow,

Fly away

Over the hills

And far away.

SUGGESTION: Ask children what their favorite weather is: sunshine? snow? fog? wind? rain? hail? Have the whole class insert these weather words into the chant. Putting the chant in a pocket chart allows children to focus on the word substitutions and title changes. Or replace *snow, snow* with two blank spaces on a photocopied version, have children write their favorite weather words in the spaces, and take the chant home to share with family members.

Snowman

This is a snowman as round as a ball.

He has two large eyes, but he's not very tall.

If the sun shines down on him today,

My jolly snowman will melt away.

SUGGESTION: Have the children be snowmen. They stand and hold arms to form a circle. At the appropriate time, they point to their eyes, point to the sun, and then fall slowly to the floor. Compare this poem to "Six Little Snowmen" (in this volume).

Soda Bread

Soda bread and soft bread,

Crazy bread and hard bread,

Loaf bread, cornbread,

Plain bread and biscuits.

SUGGESTION: *Bread* is a familiar concept for almost all children, but they may not be aware of all the varieties of bread and may not know that biscuits are a kind of bread. Make a list (using interactive writing) of many different kinds of bread, including the breads in the poem but many more—sourdough, wheat, oatmeal, French—whatever children generate. If needed, talk about the concept of a *loaf*.

fold
here

The Squirrel

Whisky, frisky,

Hippety hop,

Up he scrambles

To the treetop.

Whirly, furly,

What a tail!

Tall as a feather,

Broad as a sail!

Where's his supper?

In the shell.

Snappity, crackity—

Out it fell!

SUGGESTION: Invite children to pick out their favorite descriptive (onomatopoetic!) words from the poem, such as *whisky, frisky, whirly, furly, snappity, crackity,* and play with altering their voice—high or low pitched, softer or louder. To share further images of a squirrel, read Beatrix Potter's *Squirrel Nutkin.* Squirrels in this classic story use their tails to help them sail across the water.

Star Light, Star Bright

Star light, star bright,

First star I see tonight.

I wish I may, I wish I might

Have this wish I wish tonight.

SUGGESTION: Children love telling their wishes and illustrating them as they say the poem. Have them draw the night sky. Point out that every line has a rhyming word at the end, and ask children to say *bright*, *tonight*, and *might*.

fold here

Stretch Up High

Stretch, stretch, away up high.

On your tiptoes, reach the sky.

See the bluebirds flying high.

Now bend down and touch your toes.

Now sway as the North Wind blows.

Waddle as the gander goes.

ACTIONS:
Stretch, stretch, away up high. [*reach arms upward*]
On your tiptoes, reach the sky. [*stand on tiptoes and reach*]
See the bluebirds flying high. [*wave hands*]
Now bend down and touch your toes. [*bend to touch toes*]
Now sway as the North Wind blows. [*move body back and forth*]
Waddle as the gander goes. [*walk in waddling motion*]

fold
here

SUGGESTION: Have children say the poem with actions. This action rhyme is a good transition activity that will give children a moment of exercise before settling down again.

A Sunshiny Shower

A sunshiny shower

Won't last half an hour.

SUGGESTION: Ask children if they have ever seen the sun out when it's raining. Discuss the concept of a short sunny shower, and talk about descriptive words, such as *sunshiny*. Work together to come up with some other expressive weather words—*rainy, messy, cloudy, muddy,* and so on. Create new weather couplets about a cool wind, wet rain, or soft snow.

fold
here

239

Swim Little Fishie

Swim little fishie

Swim around the pool.

Swim little fishie

The water is cool.

Where's the little fishie?

Where did he go?

There he is!

Splash!

SUGGESTION: Children may make swimming motions with hands while saying the first four lines slowly. Then change the tone at the fifth line, looking for the fish and talking more quickly, ending with *splash!* and a wide motion of the hands.

Swim, Swan, Swim

Swan swam over the sea,

Swim, swan, swim!

Swan swam back again,

Well swum, swan!

SUGGESTION: Go on a "scavenger hunt" and find all the *sw* words. Decide which of these are action words. Help children stress particular words in order to convey the meaning.

fold
here

241

Ten Fat Sausages

Ten fat sausages sizzling in the pan,

Ten fat sausages sizzling in the pan.

One went POP! and another went BAM!

There were eight fat sausages sizzling in the pan.

ADDITIONAL VERSES:

Eight fat sausages sizzling in the pan,
Eight fat sausages sizzling in the pan.
One went POP! and another went BAM!
There were six fat sausages sizzling in the pan.

Six fat sausages sizzling in the pan,
Six fat sausages sizzling in the pan.
One went POP! and another went BAM!
There were four fat sausages sizzling in the pan.

Four fat sausages sizzling in the pan,
Four fat sausages sizzling in the pan.
One went POP! and another went BAM!
There were two fat sausages sizzling in the pan.

Two fat sausages sizzling in the pan,
Two fat sausages sizzling in the pan.
One went POP! and another went BAM!
There were no fat sausages sizzling in the pan.

SUGGESTION: There is a lot of action in this poem. That makes it interesting to illustrate as well as pantomime. *BAM!* is the part children enjoy most when they perform the actions indicated. Emphasize the *s* and *z* sounds of *sizzling* so children get the idea how these sausages sound when they cook. Start with ten fat sausages drawn on a whiteboard and subtract (erase) two at a time. Children enjoy coming up with the math equations for the disappearing sausages. This is a good poem to revisit in a pocket chart also.

Thank You

My hands say thank you
With a clap, clap, clap.
My feet say thank you
With a tap, tap, tap.

Clap, clap, clap,
Tap, tap, tap.
I turn around,
Touch the ground,
And with a bow,
I say…Thank you, now.

ACTIONS:

My hands say thank you
With a clap, clap, clap. [*clap hands three times*]
My feet say thank you
With a tap, tap, tap. [*tap one toe three times*]

Clap, clap, clap, [*clap hands*]
Tap, tap, tap. [*tap toe*]
I turn around, [*turn around*]
Touch the ground, [*squat down to touch the ground*]
And with a bow, [*bow*]
I say…Thank you, now.

SUGGESTION: Have children say the rhyme with the motions. When children know the poem, they can locate or highlight the words with the *-ap* phonogram. This poem is good for locating high frequency words.

There Are Seven Days

There are seven days

There are seven days

There are seven days in a week.

Sunday, Monday,

Tuesday, Wednesday,

Thursday, Friday, Saturday.

SUGGESTION: Sing to the tune of "Clementine" and repeat several times.

There Once Was a Sow

There once was a sow

Who had three piglets,

Three little piglets had she.

And the old sow always went, "Umph,"

And the piglets went, "Wee, wee, wee."

SUGGESTION: Children can discuss the idea that the *sow* is the mother pig and the *piglets* are the babies.

fold
here

245

There Was an Old Lady Who Swallowed a Fly

There was an old lady who swallowed a fly.

I don't know why she swallowed the fly.

Perhaps she'll die.

There was an old lady who swallowed a spider

That wriggled and jiggled and tickled inside her.

She swallowed the spider to catch the fly.

I don't know why she swallowed the fly.

Perhaps she'll die.

ADDITIONAL VERSES:

There was an old lady who swallowed a bird.
How absurd! She swallowed a bird.

She swallowed the bird to catch . . .
etc.

There was an old lady who swallowed a cat.
Think of that! She swallowed a cat.

She swallowed the cat to catch . . .
etc.

There was an old lady who swallowed a dog.
What a hog! She swallowed a dog.

She swallowed the dog to catch . . .
etc.

There was an old lady who swallowed a goat.
It stuck in her throat! She swallowed a goat.

She swallowed the goat to catch . . .
etc.

There was an old lady who swallowed a horse.
She died, of course.

SUGGESTION: Make an old lady from an open paper bag by adding arms, legs, and a head. Let children draw and cut out all the things the old lady ate. They love to feed her, stuffing the bag and chanting the rhyme.

There Was an Old Man of Peru

There was an old man of Peru

Who dreamed he was eating his shoe.

He woke in the night

In a terrible fright,

And found it was perfectly true.

SUGGESTION: Call attention to the rhymes at the ends of lines 1, 2, and 5 and lines 3 and 4 by having the children clap their hands or snap their fingers on the rhyming words. Have the children substitute other people, places, and actions to create another limerick.

There Was an Old Person of Ware

by Edward Lear

There was an old person of Ware,

Who rode on the back of a bear;

Then they asked, "Does it trot?"

He said, "Certainly not!

He's a Moppsikon Floppsikon bear!"

SUGGESTION: This is another limerick that will be entertaining. Invite children to compare it to "There Was an Old Man of Peru" both in number of rhymes and in the rhythm of the verse. They will gradually internalize the form of the limerick.

There's a Hole in the Middle of the Sea

There's a hole in the middle of the sea
There's a hole in the middle of the sea
There's a hole, there's a hole
There's a hole in the middle of the sea

There's a log in the hole in the middle of the sea
There's a log in the hole in the middle of the sea
There's a log, there's a log
There's a log in the hole in the middle of the sea

There's a bump on the log in the hole
In the middle of the sea
There's a bump on the log in the hole
In the middle of the sea
There's a bump, there's a bump
There's a bump on the log in the hole
In the middle of the sea

ADDITIONAL VERSES:
There's a frog on the bump on the log … etc.
There's a fly on the frog on the bump on the log … etc.
There's a wing on the fly on the frog … etc.
There's a flea on the wing on the fly … etc.

SUGGESTION: This cumulative rhyme can go on for many verses. The more characteristics you add, the more will be required of children's memories. Use judgment in adding verses, perhaps adding more over time.

There's Music in a Hammer

There's music in a hammer.

There's music in a nail.

There's music in a kitty cat

When you step upon her tail.

SUGGESTION: Ask children to think about the kind of *music* that a cat might make when you step on her tail. They can make the noises they think might occur. They can also discuss what is meant by the *music* in a hammer (the beat) or in a nail when you hit it.

Thirty Days Has September

Thirty days has September,

April, June, and November.

February has twenty-eight alone

All the rest have thirty-one.

Excepting leap year, that's the time

When February's days are twenty-nine.

SUGGESTION: This traditional calendar rhyme may be helpful to children all of their lives! Use it each month as you look at a calendar and see how many days there are.

fold here

251

This Little Hand

This little hand is a boy.

This little hand is his brother.

Together, they wash and they wash and they wash.

One hand washes the other.

SUGGESTION: Have children hold up one hand, then the other, and then pantomime washing their hands. Prepare poetry charts of the masculine and feminine versions of the text surrounded by children's illustrations and post them near the classroom or bathroom sinks.

This Old Man

This old man,

He can shake,

Shake, shake, shake,

While baking a cake.

Knick-knack paddy-wack,

Give your dog a bone,

Shaking, shaking,

All the way home.

ADDITIONAL VERSES:

This old man,
He can kick,
Kick, kick, kick,
Just for a trick.
Knick-knack paddy-wack,
Give your dog a bone,
Kicking, kicking,
All the way home.

This old man,
He can twist,
Twist, twist, twist,
While shaking his fist.
Knick-knack paddy-wack,
Give your dog a bone,
Twisting, twisting,
All the way home.

SUGGESTION: This is a revised version of the traditional "This Old Man." It offers children the opportunity to notice rhyming words that have the same phonogram as well as what happens when you add *ing* to words.

Three Elephants

One elephant went out to play

Upon a spider's web one day.

He thought it such a tremendous stunt

That he called for another little elephant.

Two elephants went out to play

Upon a spider's web one day.

They thought it such a tremendous stunt

That they called for another little elephant.

Three elephants went out to play

Upon a spider's web one day.

The web went CREAK, the web went CRACK,

And all of a sudden they all ran back.

SUGGESTION: First graders enjoy being elephants and walking a spider-web tightrope. Just place a piece of yarn on the floor, and increasing numbers of elephants can take this imaginary trip as other children say or sing the poem. The favorite moment comes when the web goes *CREAK* and *CRACK* and the elephants all run back to the starting place. You can substitute words such as *enormous* and *gigantic* for *tremendous* to expand vocabulary.

Three Jolly Gentlemen

Three jolly gentlemen

In coats of red

Rode their horses

Up to bed.

Three jolly gentlemen

Snored till morn,

Their horses chomping

The golden corn.

Three jolly gentlemen

At break of day

Came clitter-clatter down the stairs

And galloped away.

Three Little Bugs

Three little bugs in a basket,

Hardly room for two.

One like Mary, one like Tom,

And one that looks like you.

SUGGESTION: Children can substitute names of classmates as they recite the poem. Create a *basket* by making a circle of yarn on the floor and putting children's names in the middle.

Three Wise Men of Gotham

Three wise men of Gotham

Went to sea in a bowl;

If the bowl had been stronger,

My song would have been longer.

SUGGESTION: Ask children to puzzle out why this poem ends so abruptly. They will enjoy the joke when they figure out that the bowl sank. Invite them to make before and after pictures (this will help English-language learners with tricky words such as *wise men* and *bowl*).

fold
here

Tick-Tock

"Tick-tock, tick-tock,

Tick-tock," says the clock.

Little boy, little girl,

Time to wash our hands.

SUGGESTION: You can change this poem to fit any routine that you have established in the classroom. For example, *Time to read* or *Time for lunch*.

Tingalayo

Refrain

>Tingalayo come, little donkey, come.
>Tingalayo come, little donkey, come.

Me donkey fast, me donkey slow,
Me donkey come and me donkey go.

Refrain

Me donkey hee, me donkey haw,
Me donkey sleep in a bed of straw.

Refrain

Me donkey dance, me donkey sing,
Me donkey wearin' a diamond ring.

Refrain

Me donkey swim, me donkey ski,
Me donkey dress elegantly.

SUGGESTION: Sing the song, repeating the refrain each time. Create new verses together and sing them.

A Tiny Seed

Tiny seed planted just right,

Not a breath of air, not a ray of light.

Rain falls slowly to and fro,

And now the seed begins to grow.

Slowly reaching for the light,

With all its energy, all its might.

The little seed's work is almost done,

To grow up tall and face the sun.

SUGGESTION: Have the children roll up in a ball and then start to unfold as the seed begins to grow. At the end of the poem, they can stand up tall and stretch their arms.

To Bed, To Bed

To bed, to bed,

Says sleepy-head.

Tarry a while,

Says Slow.

Put on the pan,

Says Greedy Nan,

We'll sup before we go.

SUGGESTION: Talk with the children about the words *tarry*, meaning *stay*, and *sup*, meaning *supper*.

fold
here

261

Tom, Tom, the Piper's Son

Tom, he was a piper's son,

He learned to play when he was young;

But the only tune that he could play

Was "Over the Hills and Far Away."

Now Tom with his pipe made such a noise,

That he pleased all the girls and boys;

And they stopped to hear him play

"Over the Hills and Far Away."

SUGGESTION: Discuss the idea of a *pipe* being a musical instrument such as a flute, a clarinet, or a recorder. Ask children to listen to you read the poem and to pick out the rhyming words. Then invite them to clap the rhyming words.

Tommy Snooks

As Tommy Snooks and Bessy Brooks

Were walking out one Sunday,

Said Tommy Snooks to Bessy Brooks,

"Tomorrow will be Monday."

SUGGESTION: Invite one child to read the dialogue. You can substitute other days of the week as well as children's first and last names for *Tommy Snooks* and *Bessy Brooks*.

Traffic Safety

Red light says stop.

Green light says go.

Yellow says be careful,

You'd better go slow.

When I reach a crossing place,

To left and right I turn my face,

And then I walk, not run, across the street,

And use my head to guide my feet.

SUGGESTION: Assign particular children to read *stop*, *go*, and *be careful, you'd better go slow*. Have the children turn their heads to the left and then to the right to parallel the words.

Tweedle-dum and Tweedle-dee

Tweedle-dum and Tweedle-dee

Were set to have a battle,

For Tweedle-dum said Tweedle-dee

Had tried to tell a tattle.

Just then flew by a monstrous crow,

Who wasn't too polite.

It frightened both the heroes so,

They quite forgot to fight.

SUGGESTION: This humorous story will be interesting to first graders, especially since *tattling* is something they often do or try not to do. Have half the class read the first stanza and the other half read the second stanza.

fold
here

265

Twenty White Horses

Twenty white horses

Upon a red hill;

Now they tramp,

Now they chomp,

Now they stand still.

SUGGESTION: Children enjoy riddles and wordplay. Let them take the lead in discovering the meaning of *red hill*, *tramp*, and *chomp*. They will love discovering that the *white horses* are teeth!

Two Cats of Kilkenny

There once were two cats of Kilkenny.

Each thought there was one cat too many;

So they fought and they fit,

And they scratched and they bit,

Till, excepting their nails,

And the tips of their tails,

Instead of two cats, there weren't any.

SUGGESTION: This is a good rhyme to turn into a prose version. Children can dictate a concise retelling, which you can
write at the bottom of the chart. For example: *Two cats fought each other until there wasn't anything left of them.*

Two Crows

There were two crows sat on a stone,

Fal-de-ral, fal-de-ral.

One flew away and there was one,

Fal-de-ral, fal-de-ral.

The other seeing his neighbor gone,

Fal-de-ral, fal-de-ral.

He flew away and then there were none,

Fal-de-ral, fal-de-ral.

SUGGESTION: When you say *fal-de-ral* the first time, say it quickly. Then pace the second *fal-de-ral* more deliberately and slowly with a steady rhythm. Children will understand that the first, third, fifth, and seventh lines really tell a story and that *fal-de-ral* is added to make the poem more interesting.

Two Little Dogs

Two little dogs sat by the fire

In a basket of coal dust.

Says one little dog to the other little dog,

If you don't speak, then I must.

SUGGESTION: Explain to children that people sometimes make fires with coal—black rocks that burn but leave dust. The little dogs are sitting in the coal basket by the fire. You can compare the words *dust* and *must*.

fold
here

269

Up in the Green Orchard

Up in the green orchard there is a green tree,

The finest of pippins that you may see.

The apples are ripe and ready to fall,

And Robin and Richard shall gather them all.

SUGGESTION: Once children know that *pippins* are green apples, they'll understand why this piece of land is called *the green orchard*. Substitute names of children in class for *Robin* and *Richard*. Substitute other fruit *(apricots, peaches, cherries)* for *pippins* and change the name of the orchard accordingly.

The Vowel Song

The vowels of the alphabet

I know them all by name, oh!

a–e–i–o–u

a–e–i–o–u

a–e–i–o–u

I know them all by name, oh!

SUGGESTION: Sing to the tune of "B–I–N–G–O," repeating five more times. Each time, insert a clap for a vowel.

Way Down South

Way down south where bananas grow,

A grasshopper stepped on an elephant's toe.

The elephant said, with tears in his eyes,

"Pick on somebody your own size."

SUGGESTION: Invite children to talk about what makes this poem funny. This poem is full of contrasts as children imagine the size of an elephant and the size of a grasshopper.

What Animals Say

Bow-wow, says the dog;
Mew, mew, says the cat;
Grunt, grunt, says the hog;
And squeak, says the rat.

Chirp, chirp, says the sparrow;
Caw, caw, says the crow;
Quack, quack, says the duck;
What cuckoos say, you know.

With sparrows and cuckoos,
With rats and dogs,
With ducks and crows,
With cats and hogs,

A fine song I've made,
To please you, my dear;
And if it's well sung,
'Twill be charming to hear.

SUGGESTION: Have all the children read the verses, assigning specific children to make the sounds of each animal. If children make a cut-paper sequence of the animals on butcher paper, the artwork will help them remember what comes next. Remember to attach a printed copy of the poem to the illustration.

What Do You See?

What do you see?

A pig in a tree.

Where's your cat?

Under my hat.

How do you know?

He licked my toe.

SUGGESTION: Children love these nonsense rhymes and enjoy creating more: *What can you do? / Swim in a shoe. / Where's your chair? / Under the bear.* Children's own rhymes and illustrations make a great bulletin board display or class book. These verses also give English-language learners practice using difficult words such as *over, under, behind,* and *in front of.*

What's Your Name?

What's your name?

Puddin Tame.

Ask me again

And I'll tell you the same.

Where do you live?

In a sieve.

What's your number?

Cucumber!

SUGGESTION: Children can act out this rhyme by having half the group read the questions and the other half read the answers. This is a good poem to call children's attention to punctuation.

fold
here

275

Where Do You Wear Your Ears?

Where do you wear your ears?

Underneath your hat?

Where do you wear your ears?

Yes ma'am, just like that.

Where do you wear your ears?

Say where, you sweet, sweet child.

Where do you wear your ears?

On both ends of my smile!

SUGGESTION: This poem suggests crazy images to draw or assemble on a flannel board as the poem is recited. Have a box of felt faces, eyes, mouths, noses, ears, hair, and hats to play with on the board as you sing or recite.

Where, Oh, Where Has My Little Dog Gone?

Where, oh, where has my little dog gone?

Where, oh, where can he be?

With his ears cut short and his tail cut long,

Oh, where, oh, where can he be?

SUGGESTION: First graders can envision and describe the missing pet. Assign one third of the children to read each of the first three lines and then have everyone read the final line. Use interactive writing to make a "Lost Dog" poster.

fold
here

277

Whose Little Pigs

Whose little pigs are these, these, these?

Whose little pigs are these?

They are Roger the cook's;

I know by their looks.

I found them among my peas.

SUGGESTION: Children will enjoy this poem and may substitute other animal names for *pigs* without changing the poem in any other way. Do, however, call their attention to the title change. You may want to call attention to the word *whose* and discuss why this word means the pigs belong to someone.

Wibbleton to Wobbleton

From Wibbleton to Wobbleton is fifteen miles.

From Wobbleton to Wibbleton is fifteen miles.

From Wibbleton to Wobbleton, from Wobbleton to Wibbleton,

From Wibbleton to Wobbleton is fifteen miles.

SUGGESTION: This rhythmic verse is easy and pleasurable to say. Slow down when you say *fifteen miles*. Talk with children about this rhyme describing a journey from town to town. After children know the rhyme, call attention to the double consonants.

Wiggly Woo

There's a worm at the bottom of the garden

And his name is Wiggly Woo.

There's a worm at the bottom of the garden

And all that he can do

Is wiggle all night

And wiggle all day.

Whatever else the people say

There's a worm at the bottom of the garden

And his name is Wiggly Woo

SUGGESTION: Children can make wiggling motions with their hands as they say the rhyme. After children learn the rhyme, call attention to double consonants and vowels.

Willy Boy, Willy Boy

"Willy boy, Willy boy, where are you going?

I'll go with you, if I may."

"I'm going to the meadow to see them a-mowing,

I'm going to help them make hay."

SUGGESTION: Have half the children read the first two lines and the rest, the last two.

fold
here

281

A Wise Old Owl

by E.H. Richards

A wise old owl lived in an oak.

The more he saw, the less he spoke;

The less he spoke, the more he heard.

Why can't we all be like that wise old bird?

SUGGESTION: After one reading of the poem, ask for a volunteer to pantomime actions as the class recites [*using a hand to shade eyes and looking from side to side; covering the mouth so as not to speak; and cupping both hands behind ears*]. Then encourage a discussion about speaking and listening within a group.